CHI…
COOKBOOK

Includes turkey, duck, pheasant and quail

Ray McVinnie

David Bateman

For J. A. & G.

Other New Zealand cookbooks in this series:

Quick Smart Cookbook
No Bother Bread
The Breadwinners
Pasta Cookbook
Pasta Sauces
Mmm . . . Muffins
Cakes and Slices
Cookies and Biscuits
Microwaving Vegetables
Microwaving Main Meals
Microwaving for One or Two
Marvellous Mince
His Turn: Cooking for New Zealand Men
Potato Cookbook
Sailing and Camping Cookbook
One-dish Meals
Pizza and Quiche Cookbook
Bean Cuisine
Mmm . . . More Muffins

Published in 1994 by David Bateman Ltd, ''Golden Heights'',
34 View Road, Glenfield, Auckland, New Zealand.

ISBN 1 86953 174 4

Photography by Andrew Harvey
Cover design by Errol McLeary
Typeset by Jazz Graphics
Printed in Hong Kong by Colorcraft

Cover: Roasted pepper and chicken salad (p.15)

Contents

Introduction

I have always liked chicken, probably because I was brought up in the 1950s when it was a rare treat reserved for birthdays and Christmas.

Chicken's mild, savoury taste and white flesh have universal appeal. How many times has one been offered some new dish with the words — "Try it, it tastes just like chicken"? Fortunately, these days, chicken is readily available and relatively inexpensive (as is a growing variety of other poultry products). Perhaps its versatility is another reason for its appeal. It is used for every kind of dish, from the ultimate comfort food — chicken soup — to exotic dishes like North African B'stilla, the spiced, sugared layered filo chicken and egg pie.

There are no grand restaurant dishes here. I find I do not have time for involved cookery outside the sphere of the restaurant, yet I enjoy cooking interesting dishes at home for family and friends, and want maximum effect for minimum effort. I think you will find that all the recipes in this book fulfil this need.

It is worth remembering that a simple recipe sometimes needs more careful cooking than a complicated one, as any faults in the cooking are more easily noticed.

This eclectic gathering is the best of what has served me well and satisfied my family and friends over the years.

Abbreviations used

t	teaspoon	kg	kilogram
T	tablespoon	cm	centimetre
c	cup	g	gram
C	Celsius	L	litre
ml	millilitre		

General Information

Types of chicken
Capons — young cockerels fattened for the table (2–4 kg). Best slowly roasted or poached.
Boilers — chickens over 12 months old (2–3 kg). Good for broths, mousses, cold dishes, or served with or in a sauce. Meaty, but sometimes salty.
Roasters — (1–2 kg) most popular. Roast, boil or pot roast.
Spring chickens — broilers, about 3 months old (1–5 kg). Good for sautéing or frying.
Poussins — baby chickens, 4–6 weeks old, usually only enough for one person. Grill or fry quickly; or stuff well and roast quickly.

Duck
Unless you shoot a wild duck, most ducks available are raised commercially and frozen. They have a large frame and a high fat content, but not a lot of meat.

Turkey
Available fresh but usually bought frozen from the supermarket. Turkey breasts are also available. Cook carefully as they can be dry.

Quail
Available fresh from speciality shops (as are the eggs).

Pheasant
Usually not very big and can be dry though, if cooked carefully, they are one of the most delicious types of poultry and game.

Guinea fowl
Flesh is tender and gamey, similar to pheasant. Can replace pheasant in recipes.

Jointing poultry and game birds
Hold bird firmly on a board. With a sharp knife, cut away skin between leg and breast. Press flat side of the knife against the carcass, hold leg and bend it outwards until oyster bone breaks away from the carcass.

Slide knife around the leg joint, cutting down towards the "parson's nose", keeping it between oyster and back bone. The leg is now severed from the carcass and has the oyster bone attached. Repeat for the other leg.

Make a slantwise cut with a knife halfway up the breast, across the top of the wishbone, from neck to end of the wing joint. Cut through the wishbone and ribs to detach the wing with a good portion of the breast.

Twist the wing pinion out and tuck it under the breast meat; this holds the joint flat for cooking. Repeat for the other wing and breast.

Cut away the breast meat in one piece.

These are the joints — all that is left are the ribs, backbone and "parson's nose".

Boning poultry and game birds

Slit the skin down the underside of the birds, work the skin and flesh from the carcass with a knife until the leg joint is reached.

Nick sinew of ball and socket joint between thigh bone and carcass. Hold onto the end of the joint in one hand and, working from the inside of the leg, cut away the flesh. Scrape thigh bone clean.

Continue to clean the drumstick until the whole leg is free of flesh. Remove the leg bone from the carcass. Repeat for the other leg.

Sever the wing joint from the carcass. Using a knife, work down towards and onto the breastbone. Stop. Repeat on other wing.

Carefully cut away the skin from the top of the breastbone. Do not puncture the skin. Keep both sides of the chicken attached to the skin.

Lay bird flat ready for stuffing, etc.

Stocks and Soups

Chicken stock

As chicken stock is the basis for many sauces and soups, it is worth knowing how to make it. Of course you can use dried commercial stock, but homemade is a better product and can be made from parts of the chicken which are usually discarded. Save raw carcasses and bones by freezing until you have enough for a pot of stock, and then freeze your homemade stock.

A large lump of frozen chicken stock thrown into a pot with a few fresh ingredients may not sound too appetising, but it can soon be turned into a satisfying homemade soup or stew. This is what you need:

2 kg raw chicken carcasses, bones, necks, wing tips
1 leek, well washed and chopped
2 carrots, chopped
2 onions, peeled and chopped
1 stalk celery, chopped

Put all ingredients into a large stock pot, cover with cold water and bring to the boil. Simmer for 3 hours, skimming off any scum that collects. (Do not add salt, this is done later when the stock is used in a soup or stew). Strain, discarding the vegetables and bones. Cool. Leave overnight in the refrigerator and then skim off any fat. The stock should have "jellied". It will keep for about a week in the refrigerator and much longer if frozen. Do not refreeze.

Vegetable stock

A good standby if you have no chicken scraps.

450 g carrots
450 g onions
½ head celery
25 g butter
4 peppercorns
1 t tomato purée
1200 ml water
salt to taste

Chop vegetables roughly, brown lightly in butter, add remaining ingredients. Bring to the boil, and then simmer for 2 hours or until the stock has a good flavour. Strain carefully and refrigerate.

Note: If you want a clear stock, the secret is to simmer, not boil, and remove any scrum as it rises.

Chicken broth with Parmesan and eggs (Stracciatella) ***(serves 4)***

This Italian soup is a great standby — quick, inexpensive and very good.

4 eggs
5 T grated Parmesan cheese
1 L well-flavoured chicken stock

Break eggs into a bowl. Add the cheese and beat well until thick and creamy. Bring stock to the boil, taste, and boost the flavour with a little dried chicken stock if necessary. The broth needs to be well-flavoured.

Pour the egg and cheese mixture into the boiling stock, beating vigorously with a whisk so the eggs do not stick together. Serve immediately.

Egg flower soup ***(serves 4)***

A Chinese version of the previous soup. Just omit the cheese and add a few drops of soy sauce to each soup bowl before serving. Garnish with chopped spring onions.

Chicken broth with fresh pasta ***(serves 4)***

1 L well-flavoured chicken stock
250 g fresh linguini or fettucine
1 whole chicken breast, boned, skinned and finely chopped
2 spring onions, finely chopped
2 T finely chopped parsley
4 T grated Parmesan cheese

Bring the stock to the boil, add pasta and continue boiling until the pasta rises to the top. It should be just cooked. Add chicken meat, spring onions and parsley. Bring back to the boil and give the soup a good stir. Serve immediately. Garnish each bowl of soup with 1 T grated Parmesan.

Chicken and sweetcorn soup *(serves 4)*

500 ml chicken stock
1 c creamed sweetcorn
½ c finely chopped chicken meat, raw or cooked
2 finely chopped spring onions
1 T soy sauce

Combine all ingredients in a heavy-based saucepan. Bring slowly to the boil, simmer for 2 or 3 minutes, taste and season with salt and pepper. If the soup is too thick, thin with a little chicken stock or milk.

Chicken and mushroom purée *(serves 4)*

50 g butter
1 T chopped fresh tarragon
2 T chopped parsley
2 cloves garlic, crushed
1 large onion, peeled and roughly chopped
1 carrot, peeled and chopped
250 g mushrooms, chopped
1 chicken (about 1 kg), jointed
juice ½ lemon
200 ml white wine
1 L chicken stock or water
150 ml cream

In a large saucepan, melt the butter until it is hot but not burning. Add tarragon, parsley, garlic, onion, carrot and mushrooms, and cook over a low heat for 5 minutes. Do not allow to brown. Add chicken pieces and cook for another 5 minutes, turning frequently.

Add lemon juice and wine, stir, and simmer for 2 minutes. Add chicken stock or water and bring to the boil. Reduce heat and simmer for 45 minutes or until the meat is falling off the bones.

Discard bones and cartilage. Purée the mixture in a food processor or blender, or pass through a sieve several times. Add cream and season with salt and pepper. Serve with French bread.

Chicken, leek and almond soup *(serves 4)*

50 g butter
1 small onion, finely chopped
3 leeks, well washed and thinly sliced
150 g almonds, roasted and roughly chopped
250 g skinned, boneless chicken meat, thinly sliced
50 ml white wine
1 L well-flavoured chicken stock (dried will do)
salt, pepper and lemon juice to taste
1 T chopped parsley
cream

In a large saucepan, melt the butter but do not let it burn. Add onion, leeks, almonds and chicken meat. Fry gently for 5 minutes until the vegetables are soft and golden but not brown. Add wine and boil for 1 minute, then add stock and simmer for 10 minutes. Remove from heat, purée in a blender or food processor, or sieve. Taste and season with salt, pepper and lemon juice. Add parsley. Serve with a little cream poured over each serving.

Instant oriental chicken soup *(serves 4)*

This recipe was given to me by an old friend. She says: "I discovered this one winter evening when I had that dreaded combination of bored tastebuds and felt too lazy to cook. The freshness and smell was a revelation! Even better if you have a few coriander leaves on hand."

4 c well-flavoured chicken stock
2 c vegetables (broccoli, carrots, mushrooms, celery, fresh ginger) cut into thin strips
200 g skinned, boneless chicken, very thinly sliced
3 T soy sauce
chilli sauce, if desired

Bring stock to a fast boil. Add all ingredients and bring back to the boil. Serve immediately. The chicken will be cooked and the vegetables "al dente".

Green peas with chicken and bacon *(serves 4)*

This is a hearty soup that is almost a stew.

50 g butter
1 clove garlic, crushed
1 T chopped parsley
½ onion, finely chopped
3 rashers bacon, cut into 3-cm dice
1 whole small chicken breast, finely sliced
50 ml white wine
1½ c green peas (frozen will do)
1 L chicken stock

Melt butter in a heavy saucepan. Add garlic, parsley, onion and bacon, and fry gently for 3 minutes or until golden. Add chicken, let it colour, then add wine. Boil for 1 minute. Add peas and boil for another minute. Pour in stock, bring to the boil and simmer for 5 minutes. Season with salt and pepper. Garnish with grated Parmesan cheese. Serve with French bread.

Chicken soup with glass noodles *(serves 4)*

1.5 L well-flavoured chicken stock
1 whole chicken breast, skinned and sliced very thinly
100 g Lungkow bean thread noodles, soaked in boiling water for 30 minutes, then drained
1 t ginger, finely chopped
2 cloves garlic, finely chopped
1 t lemon grass, finely chopped
1 t coriander leaves
1 small chilli, finely sliced
pinch turmeric
6 spinach leaves
2 spring onions, chopped
Kikkoman soy sauce

Bring chicken stock to the boil, add all other ingredients and bring back to the boil. Ladle into deep soup bowls. Serve with chopsticks, and soy sauce on the side.

Salads

Duck and papaya salad *(serves 4)*

500 g leftover roast duck, sliced
6 sticks celery, thinly sliced
¼ medium papaya, peeled, seeded and chopped into 2-cm cubes
100 g almonds, toasted and chopped
2 oranges, peeled, cored and sliced
2 T chopped chives
100 ml vinaigrette (made from 6 parts oil, 1 part wine vinegar, salt and black pepper)
celery leaves

Put all ingredients into a large shallow bowl and pour on enough vinaigrette to coat well. Toss the salad and decorate with celery leaves. Serve with French bread.

Turkey and apple salad *(serves 4)*

1 lettuce heart
500 g cooked turkey breast, sliced
2 eating apples, sliced thinly around the core and sprinkled with lemon juice to prevent browning
1 c ricotta cheese
2 sticks celery, sliced thinly
50 ml vinaigrette (p.17)
2 T chopped parsley
extra chopped parsley

In a large shallow bowl, make a bed of lettuce leaves. In a separate bowl, carefully combine all the other ingredients. Spoon the turkey and apple mixture onto the leaves and sprinkle with extra chopped parsley.

Chicken and cream cheese salad *(serves 4)*

1.5-kg chicken, cooked and thinly chopped
1 lettuce, washed and torn into large pieces
2 tomatoes, cored and cut into small wedges
5 gherkins, finely sliced
1 T green peppercorns
250 g cream cheese
vinaigrette (p.17)

Combine all the ingredients, except vinaigrette, in a salad bowl, spooning the cheese in small blobs through the other ingredients. Dress with vinaigrette and toss the salad a few times. Serve with French bread.

Smoked chicken and pecan salad *(serves 4)*

The bitterness of the endive is excellent with the saltiness of the chicken and sweetness of the oranges, while the pecans make the chicken rich.

3 smoked chicken breasts (halves), skinned and thinly chopped
1 c roasted pecans
2 spring onions, finely chopped
2 oranges, peeled and thinly sliced
2 heads curly endive, washed, with leaves detached from the core
50 ml vinaigrette (made with wine vinegar and 1 t seed mustard)

Combine all ingredients in a bowl and dress liberally with vinaigrette.

Cold roast chicken with melon *(serves 4)*

2-kg roasting chicken
50 g butter
2–3 cloves garlic
lemon juice
1 large honeydew or rock melon, chilled
juice ½ orange
juice 1 lemon
2 T chopped parsley
freshly ground black pepper

Preheat oven to 200°C. Roast the chicken in the butter, with the garlic cloves inside the bird and a good squeeze of lemon juice over it. Baste often as it is cooking (for about 1½ hours) until it is well browned. When it is cooked, remove from oven and allow to cool completely. (You can cook the chicken the day before.)

Remove all the meat from the chicken, including the skin. Slice coarsely and set aside.

Peel the melon and cut into 3-cm cubes. Place in a large bowl with the chicken meat and squeeze the orange juice and lemon juice over the mixture. Sprinkle on chopped parsley and plenty of pepper. Toss thoroughly and serve.

Beetroot and turkey salad *(serves 4)*

4 beetroots, washed, with green tops cut off about 1 cm away from the beetroot itself. (Do not puncture the skin.)
500 g roast turkey meat, chopped
4 sticks celery, thinly sliced
1 T fresh tarragon leaves
50 ml vinaigrette (p.17) (plus 1 dessertspoon seed mustard and 1 clove garlic)

Put beetroots into a baking dish and bake them dry (do not add any oil or fat to the dish) for 1 hour or until they are completely soft. Allow to cool, then skin them and cut into 3-cm cubes. Combine with turkey, celery and tarragon in a bowl, and dress with the vinaigrette.

Quail and lettuce salad *(serves 4)*

olive oil for frying
4 quails, cut in half lengthways
salt and freshly ground pepper
150 ml vinaigrette (p.17) (with 2 dessertspoons rum, clove of garlic and juice ½ orange)
1 large iceberg or cos lettuce, washed
chopped parsley

In a large frying pan, heat the olive oil until hot. Add the quail halves and fry until they are cooked through, browned and crisp. Remove from pan and drain. Place in a shallow bowl and season with salt and freshly ground black pepper. Pour on vinaigrette and leave in a cool place.

Tear up the lettuce and make a bed of lettuce in a serving bowl. Arrange the quail on top and dress with the vinaigrette in which the quail were cooling. Sprinkle with chopped parsley. Serve with French bread, and eat the quail with your fingers.

Warm chicken and potato salad *(serves 4)*

6 medium potatoes, cut into 3-cm cubes (skin can be left on)
500 g cooked chicken meat, thinly chopped
3 anchovy fillets, finely chopped
1 T capers
4 gherkins, roughly chopped
2 T chopped chives
2 sticks celery, thinly sliced
1 c mayonnaise (p.19)

Boil the potatoes, then drain and combine with all other ingredients in a salad bowl. (The heat of the potatoes will warm everything up.) Stir well and serve immediately.

Virginia chicken and apple salad *(serves 4)*

1 lettuce, washed and torn up
2 c chopped, cooked chicken meat
1 c unpeeled, cored apple cubes, about 2-cm dice
1 c sliced celery
½ c stuffed olives
½ c chopped roasted almonds
½ c mayonnaise (p.19)
½ c whipped cream
juice ½ lemon
2 T chopped parsley
salt and pepper
young celery leaves, extra olives and apple slices

In a salad bowl, make a bed of lettuce. Combine all other ingredients and season with salt and pepper. Place the mixture on the lettuce leaves and decorate with young celery leaves, extra olives and apples slices dipped in lemon juice.

Chicken, grape and almond salad ***(serves 4)***

½ c mayonnaise (p.19)
½ c cream
juice 1 lemon
2 c chopped, cooked chicken meat
1 green capsicum, cored, seeded and finely sliced
⅔ c slivered roasted almonds
4 sticks celery, thinly sliced
2 c green or purple grapes
selection of greens (endive, cos lettuce, green oakleaf or butterhead)

Combine the mayonnaise, cream and lemon juice, and season well with salt and pepper. Add the other ingredients and mix well. Present the salad on a bed of greens and decorate with extra grapes and nuts.

Roasted pepper and chicken salad
(illustrated front cover) ***(serves 4)***

10 x 2-cm thick slices of French bread, toasted on each side
2-kg chicken roasted with plenty of olive oil, garlic, pepper and salt. Baste well during cooking so skin is browned and crisp
6 large tomatoes, skinned, cored and thickly sliced
6 large red capsicums baked in a very hot oven until the skin blackens and bubbles. Wash skin off under running water, then core and de-seed them. Slice thinly
chopped parsley

Dressing
150 ml olive oil
25 ml wine vinegar
2 cloves garlic, crushed
1 T paprika
1 T sugar
1 T tomato paste
salt and pepper

Blend all the dressing ingredients. To assemble the salad, put a layer of toasted bread on a serving platter, then a layer of chicken meat, then tomatoes, then capsicum. Pour on all the dressing and let the salad sit at room temperature for half an hour. Sprinkle with chopped parsley before serving.

Chicken and lime salad *(serves 4)*

- 1 c black olives
- 2 limes, thinly sliced
- 1 telegraph cucumber, cut into 2-cm cubes, skin on
- 4 tomatoes, cored and cut into wedges
- 2 c button mushrooms
- ½ French loaf, cut into bite-sized portions
- 1.5-kg chicken boiled, skinned, boned and meat chopped roughly
- 1 t cracked black peppercorns
- 2 T chopped parsley
- 150 ml vinaigrette (p.17)

Mix all ingredients and dress salad with vinaigrette.

Thai-esque chicken salad *(serves 4)*

- 1 kg boned chicken meat (thighs or breasts)
- 1 small iceberg lettuce, washed and torn up
- 3 tomatoes, cut into wedges
- ½ telegraph cucumber, sliced
- 3 green chillis, sliced thinly
- ½ c mint leaves
- ½ c basil leaves
- ½ c coriander leaves
- 4 spring onions, thinly sliced diagonally
- 1 c roasted peanuts, roughly chopped
- lime or lemon wedges

Sauce

- ½ c fresh lime juice
- 1 c Japanese soy sauce
- ½ c rice or cider vinegar
- 3 T sugar
- ½ c Thai fish sauce
- 1 T fresh ginger, finely chopped
- 1 T fresh coriander, finely chopped
- 1 green chilli, finely chopped

Mix sauce ingredients together well.

Pan fry the chicken until golden and crisp, and cooked through. Pour off any fat and pour the sauce over the hot chicken. Leave to stand for 5 minutes.

In the meantime, in a large bowl, make a bed of lettuce. Sprinkle on the tomatoes and cucumber. Slice the chicken finely and reheat in the sauce if it has gone cold. Scatter the chicken over the salad. Reserve the sauce. Sprinkle the chillis, herbs and spring onions over the chicken. Pour on the hot sauce and sprinkle on the peanuts. Garnish with lemon or lime wedges and serve.

Sauces, Marinades and Stuffings

Soy marinade for chicken

This is good for chicken that is to be barbecued, baked or fried.

50 ml soy sauce
50 ml soya bean oil
25 ml sherry
1 T grated root ginger
2 T chopped fresh coriander
1 T honey
2 cloves garlic, crushed

Combine all ingredients well and marinate the chicken for 2–3 hours, or longer, before cooking.

Yoghurt marinade for chicken

200 ml plain yoghurt
juice 1 lemon
4 cloves garlic, crushed
1 t freshly ground black pepper
2 sprigs rosemary, bruised

Combine all ingredients and marinate the pieces overnight, if possible.

Sandra's barbecue marinade

2 T Dijon mustard
2 T Wholegrain mustard
1 T honey
50 ml Worcestershire sauce
3 cloves garlic, crushed
sprigs of rosemary, thyme or oregano

Combine all ingredients. Marinate the chicken pieces for half a day and then barbecue them, brushing with extra marinade as they cook. Serve with warmed whole kernel sweetcorn.

Basic vinaigrette

2 parts olive oil
salt and pepper
1 part cider vinegar or lemon juice

Combine all ingredients and refrigerate.

Red wine marinade for chicken or quail

This gives the meat a rich, gamey flavour.

4 bay leaves
6 juniper berries
1 small onion, peeled and sliced
2 cloves garlic, chopped
150 ml red wine
25 ml olive oil

Lay the quail or chicken pieces in a flat dish and strew the bay leaves, juniper berries, onion and garlic over them. Mix the wine and oil together and pour over everything. The longer you leave the marinade, the stronger the flavour. No less than 2 hours and no more than 2 days is recommended.

Charmoula

A chicken marinade from North America.

1 c olive oil
½ c stoned black olives, roughly chopped
4 cloves garlic, finely chopped
2 T grated fresh ginger
2 T chopped mint
2 T chopped coriander
3 green chillis, finely chopped
1 preserved lemon, finely chopped
zest and juice of 1 orange
½ t salt

Mix everything well and rub a 1.5-kg chicken all over, inside and out, with the mixture. Roast, covered, at a high heat until cooked.

Tomato salsa

This sauce is excellent with barbecued chicken or quail, plain roasted chicken or chicken breasts. It will keep for about a week in the refrigerator or it can be frozen for several months.

50 ml olive oil
3 cloves garlic, chopped
3 onions, peeled and roughly chopped
1 T sugar
¼ t cayenne pepper (more or less as desired)
2 T fresh chopped coriander
2 x 425-g cans whole peeled tomatoes in juice or 10 large tomatoes, peeled and cored

In a heavy-based saucepan, heat the olive oil until hot but not smoking. Add garlic and onions, and reduce the heat. Add sugar, cayenne and coriander, and cook on low heat, without browning, for 3–5 minutes. Stir frequently to prevent sticking. Add tomatoes and bring to the boil. Simmer for 10 minutes, stirring frequently. Taste and season with salt and pepper.

Basic mayonnaise

A well-made mayonnaise or one of its variations is an excellent accompaniment to cold chicken or turkey, or panfried chicken breasts. Mayonnaise is an emulsion of egg yolks and oil, flavoured with pepper, salt and lemon juice. It should be thick and buttery, and a golden yellow colour.

Remember to have all your ingredients and equipment at room temperature. A food processor or electric mixer is a big help.

3 egg yolks
1 t lemon juice, or wine, cider or white vinegar (not malt)
300 ml olive oil (or any other oil)

Beat the egg yolks with lemon juice or vinegar. When they have thickened a little, start adding the oil, drop by drop, beating all the time on the fastest speed, to start the emulsion. If you add the oil too fast, it will curdle. After about ⅓ of the oil has been "dropped" in, the sauce should start to look thick and fluffy. Then, and only then, increase the oil to a trickle, still beating all the time. Use all the oil, then taste and season as you would a boiled egg. Do not mistake the need for salt as a deficiency in lemon juice or vinegar.

If the sauce does curdle, do not panic, just take a clean bowl, another egg yolk, and start again with a few tablespoons of oil, drop by drop, until it emulsifies. Add the curdled mixture, drop by drop, to the new mixture, stirring continuously, and then continue adding any remaining oil, if there is any.

Aioli or garlic mayonnaise

Add 2 crushed cloves of peeled garlic to the basic recipe above.

Avocado mayonnaise

Beat an avocado to a paste and add it to the basic recipe. Season with more lemon juice and a small pinch of cayenne pepper.

Fresh herb mayonnaise

Season the basic recipe with a little garlic and finely chopped fresh herbs. The choice of herbs depends on availability and your preference. Avoid sage as it has little affinity with fresh mayonnaise.

Mustard and dill mayonnaise

Add 2 T good French mustard and 1 T chopped fresh dill to the basic recipe.

Sauce remoulade

Excellent with grilled or barbecued chicken.

3 anchovy fillets, finely chopped
1 T capers
1 T finely chopped gherkins
1 T French mustard
1 t finely chopped fresh tarragon
2 t finely chopped parsley

Combine ingredients and mix well into the basic mayonnaise recipe.

Basic sauce hollandaise

Often seen as part of the restaurant repertoire but rarely made by home cooks, which is a shame because it is easy to make, looks good, sounds impressive and always pleases.

The method described differs from that found in most cookery books, but is the one most often used by chefs because it is fast and avoids most of the pitfalls of the traditional method.

It is similar to mayonnaise in that it is an emulsion of egg yolks but, instead of oil, melted butter is used. Its consistency is rather liked whipped cream and it is golden yellow in colour. It is good with poached chicken or turkey breast.

250 g unsalted butter
juice ½ lemon
1 T white wine
3 egg yolks

Gently melt the butter and put aside. Combine lemon juice, wine and egg yolks in a large metal bowl and place over a saucepan of hot but not boiling water. Whisk over the heat until the mixture is pale yellow and frothy. It should almost double in bulk. Remove mixture from the heat and whisk in the melted butter, a little at a time, as you would the oil for mayonnaise. Season with ground white pepper and salt.

Direct heat or cold draughts will make the sauce turn, so, if you are making it ahead of time (and it lasts for several hours), be careful where you put it. If it does turn, melt the turned sauce over gentle heat until it separates completely. Put a few tablespoons of boiling water into a clean bowl and slowly add the melted sauce to the boiling water, whisking continuously, and your sauce will revive.

Sauce Béarnaise

A perfect accompaniment for fried chicken served with grilled tomatoes and salad. The method for making Béarnaise is identical to that for hollandaise (p.20), but it has a different flavour.

6 T wine vinegar
6 T white wine
1 T chopped shallot (onion will do)
2–3 stalks parsley
3 egg yolks
salt and freshly ground black pepper
2 T chopped tarragon (fresh or dried)
250 g unsalted butter

Put all ingredients into a saucepan, bring to the boil and boil until the mixture has reduced by half. Strain the mixture and save the liquid. Melt the butter, as for hollandaise. Add the reduction to the egg yolks and proceed according to the recipe for hollandaise (p.20).

When the sauce is made, add 1 T chopped fresh tarragon and 1 T chopped parsley. Adjust seasonings with salt and pepper.

Sauce verte (green sauce)

Make the basic hollandaise sauce (p.20) and add the following:

1 T finely chopped fresh tarragon
1 T chopped parsley
1 T chopped chervil
small amount lemon juice
5–6 spinach leaves, lightly cooked in boiling water, squeezed dry, cooled, chopped and puréed
salt and pepper

Cucumber and dill hollandaise

Delicious with panfried crumbed chicken breast.

Make the basic hollandaise and add the following:

1 telegraph cucumber, thinly sliced
salt
1 T finely chopped dill

Sprinkle cucumber with salt and leave for ½ hour. (This will make any bitterness disappear and soften it.) Rinse off the salt with cold water and squeeze the cucumber dry. Chop until almost a purée. Add dill to basic hollandaise with the cucumber. Taste and adjust the seasoning.

Artichoke hollandaise

Make the basic hollandaise (p.20) and add the following:

5–6 artichoke hearts	lemon juice

Thinly slice the boiled and cooled artichoke hearts (canned will do). Season with lemon juice and add to hollandaise.

Rouille

A fiery Provençal sauce, usually served with fish, but just as good with barbecued chicken pieces.

1 large clove garlic, chopped	50 ml olive oil
handful of breadcrumbs	chicken stock (optional)
1 large red capsicum	1 small red chilli, chopped

Soak breadcrumbs in water, and squeeze dry. Grill the capsicum until the skin is black and charred all over. Wash skin off under running water and discard the core and seeds. Put the capsicum, garlic and chilli into a food processor or blender with garlic/breadcrumb mixture. Blend to a paste and continue blending, adding the oil a little at a time, as for mayonnaise. Thin with chicken stock to the consistency of lightly whipped cream. Taste and season.

Apple sauce for roast turkey

3 good-sized sweet eating apples	1 T brandy or Calvados
100 g butter	lemon juice
150 ml white wine or cider	salt and pepper
150 ml cream	sugar

Peel and core the apples and cut into 1-cm dice. Gently cook in the butter in a frying pan over a low heat until they are soft and golden. Remove the apples and set aside. Add wine and cream to the pan and reduce to half by fast boiling.

Pour onto the apples and stir well. Add the brandy or Calvados. Taste and season with lemon juice, salt, pepper and sugar.

Sauce ravigote

Good with hot roast chicken or boiled potatoes.

75 ml olive oil
10 ml wine vinegar
juice ½ lemon
1 T capers
½ onion, finely chopped
1 T finely chopped tarragon
1 T finely chopped parsley
1 T finely chopped chervil
salt and pepper

Mix the oil, vinegar and lemon juice together, and add the other ingredients. Mix well and serve separately.

A South American variation is to omit the tarragon, substituting half a finely chopped green chilli.

Mango or peach chutney

Serve with cold roast chicken or turkey. Exceptionally good!

10 mangoes or 15 large peaches, green but not too hard
230 ml wine vinegar
250 g soft brown sugar
150 ml water
1 c raisins
juice and rind 1 large lemon
6 cardamom pods, pounded, skins discarded
1 T chopped fresh ginger
2 T black mustard seeds
1 T salt
¼ t grated nutmeg
½ t cayenne pepper

If using mangoes, peel six of them, cut them off the stone and slice thickly. Cut the remaining 4 off the stone, leaving the skin on. If using peaches, peel and stone them all.

Set the fruit to one side. Put all other ingredients into a large pot and bring to the boil. Simmer for 15 minutes, then add the fruit. Simmer for another 20 minutes, stirring occasionally to prevent sticking. Taste and season with more salt if necessary. Pour into sterilised jars and seal. Leave for 3 or 4 months before using.

Kumara and ginger stuffing (for 1 medium-sized chicken)

100 g butter
¼ onion, finely chopped
1 large clove garlic
1 T finely chopped fresh ginger
1 c grated kumara
2 T chopped parsley
100 g almonds, roughly chopped
100 ml white wine

Melt the butter over a low heat in a large frying pan. Add onion, garlic and ginger, and fry gently, without browning, for 2–3 minutes. Add the remaining ingredients, except for the wine and seasonings, and continue to fry them gently for 5 minutes. Add the wine and bring to the boil. Continue boiling until the liquid has almost disappeared. Take off the heat, stir well and season with salt and pepper. Cool, then stuff the chicken with the mixture and roast slowly.

Apple, prune and sage stuffing (for a 1½–2 kg bird)

2 sweet eating apples, cored and cut into 1-cm dice
½ c pitted prunes, chopped
¼ c fresh chopped sage leaves (do not use dried)
1 clove garlic, crushed
½ onion, finely chopped
50 g butter, melted
½ c fresh breadcrumbs

Preheat oven to 200°C. Mix all the ingredients and season with plenty of salt and pepper. Stuff the bird and roast for 1½–2 hours. Good for roast turkey as well.

Apricot, celery and walnut stuffing for turkey

1 c dried apricots
6 sticks celery, sliced
1 c chopped walnuts
1 large onion, finely chopped
½ c chopped parsley
1 c fresh breadcrumbs
100 g butter, melted
50 ml sherry or port
2 rashers fat bacon, cut into 1-cm dice
salt and pepper

Soak apricots in boiling water for 10 minutes, then drain and chop roughly. Blanch celery in boiling water for 2 minutes. Drain and cool.

Mix all ingredients and stuff a large turkey. Roast slowly until the bird is well cooked, basting frequently.

Pork and pistachio stuffing for chicken

This is a very rich dish and needs only boiled potatoes and one green vegetable with it.

1 c minced fat belly pork
½ c shelled pistachios, chopped roughly
1 small onion, finely chopped
1 chicken liver, finely chopped
1 t chopped thyme
50 ml port or sherry
1 t salt
2 cloves garlic, chopped
1 t sugar
1 egg

Combine all the ingredients thoroughly and stuff a medium-sized roasting chicken with the mixture. Roast in a pan with a lid, or cover with tinfoil, until the juices run clear when a skewer is pushed into the stuffing. Make a gravy from the pan juices (fat removed), with half a glass of wine and water. Thicken with a little cornflour.

Corn bread, pecan and peach stuffing

Corn bread — an American favourite — gives this stuffing its distinctive flavour. It will keep in the freezer for several months and is worth taking the trouble to make.

Corn bread

125 g coarse cornmeal
100 g white flour
50 g sugar
½ t salt
2 t baking powder
1 egg, beaten
225 ml milk
50 g butter, melted

Preheat oven to 200°C. Put dry ingredients into a bowl, add beaten egg, milk and butter, and beat until smooth. Bake in a greased tin for 25 minutes. Cool and use the next day.

Stuffing

1 c corn bread, broken into small pieces
1 large ripe peach, peeled and chopped
½ c pecans, roughly chopped
rind and juice ½ orange
25 g butter, melted
1 T chopped parsley
salt and pepper

Mix all ingredients and stuff a medium-sized chicken, duck or pheasant. Roast in a hot oven with extra butter. Serve with gravy made in the pan with the juices, water, salt and pepper, and thickened with flour or cornflour.

Rice and Pasta

Chicken livers with pasta and tomatoes (serves 4)

25 ml olive oil
500 g chicken livers, cleaned, trimmed and cut into separate lobes
1 large onion, peeled and chopped
2 cloves garlic, chopped
100 g pinenuts
2 T chopped parsley
½ c dry white wine
1 t sugar
425-g can whole peeled tomatoes in juice
500 g pasta (spaghetti, linguini or fettucine, fresh or dried)
freshly grated Parmesan cheese
chopped parsley

Heat the olive oil in a large heavy frying pan until hot, and fry the livers until they have coloured all over. Turn them without breaking them. Add onion, garlic, pinenuts and parsley, and cook for a further 3–4 minutes. Do not let the onion brown. Add wine and boil for 1 minute, then add sugar and tomatoes, and cook for another 5 minutes, simmering gently. The mixture should look thick and shiny. Break up the tomatoes with a fork. Taste and season with salt and pepper.

Cook the pasta according to packet instructions. Divide onto 4 plates, or put onto one large serving platter. Pour the chicken liver mixture over the top. Sprinkle with plenty of cheese, more chopped parsley and serve.

Gnocchi alla Romana with chicken liver sauce *(serves 6)*

This gnocchi is made from semolina. It is like fresh pasta.

Gnocchi

1 L milk
4 cloves garlic, finely chopped
¼ t grated nutmeg
50 g butter
300 g semolina
150 g Parmesan cheese, grated
2 egg yolks

Pour the milk into a large saucepan, add garlic, nutmeg and butter. Bring to the boil, then take off the heat and sprinkle in the semolina, stirring constantly. Continue stirring and put over a low heat. The mixture will become very thick. Stir in the cheese and beaten egg yolks. Season well with salt and pepper. When a wooden spoon will stand upright in the mixture, unsupported, it is ready. Spread into a greased Swiss roll tin so that it is about 2 cm thick. Leave until completely cold, then cut into 4-cm squares or use a cutter of your choice, and arrange the pieces on an ovenproof platter. Sprinkle with more cheese and dot with small pieces of butter. Put under a hot grill until browned and sizzling.

Sauce for gnocchi (serve separately)

50 g butter
1 large onion, peeled and finely chopped
1 clove garlic, finely chopped
1 T fresh chopped marjoram
500 g chicken livers, cleaned, trimmed and chopped into 2-3 cm pieces
1 c sliced mushrooms
juice ½ lemon
100 ml marsala or sweet sherry
100 ml cream
chopped parsley

In a large frying pan, melt the butter until it is hot but not brown. Fry onion until it is golden, then add garlic and marjoram, then livers and mushrooms. Fry for 3 minutes, stirring constantly. Add lemon juice and marsala or sherry. Boil for 2 minutes, then add cream. Boil for a further 2 minutes. Taste and season with salt and pepper.

Pour the mixture into a bowl and serve separately with the hot gnocchi. Garnish everything with chopped parsley.

Chicken breasts with Gorgonzola, nuts and fettucine *(serves 4)*

500 g fresh fettucine
100 g butter
1 large onion, finely chopped
2 cloves garlic, peeled and chopped
2 T chopped parsley
150 g chopped hazelnuts or almonds, or both
3 boneless chicken breasts (halves), skinned and thinly sliced
100 ml white wine or dry vermouth
150 ml cream
juice ½ lemon
½ c Italian Gorgonzola cheese, or NZ blue vein
chopped parsley

Cook pasta in boiling salted water until "al dente" and put to one side.

In a large frying pan, melt the butter until it is hot but not brown. Add onion, garlic, parsley and nuts, and stir fry for 3–4 minutes until the onion is golden. Add the chicken and stir well, cooking for 3 minutes. Add the wine and boil until the liquid has reduced by half. Add the cream and, when it comes to the boil, add the pasta and carefully turn the mixture over until it is all amalgamated and the pasta is hot. Taste and season with salt, pepper and lemon juice. Pour everything into a hot serving dish and crumble the cheese over it. Sprinkle on more chopped parsley.

Paella — Spanish chicken and seafood with rice *(serves 6)*

Traditionally, Paella is cooked in a special shallow metal casserole on top of the stove over a gentle heat with more liquid being added as it evaporates. However, I have used my usual convenient oven method.

50 ml olive oil
1 large onion, roughly chopped
1 small red capsicum, cored, seeded and chopped
1 clove garlic, finely chopped
1 large whole boneless chicken breast, sliced
3 large tomatoes, peeled, cored and seeded
1 can artichoke hearts, halved
½ c frozen peas
12 small live mussels (in the shell)
1 c cooked prawns
1 crayfish tail (if available) shelled, cooked and sliced
1 squid tube, sliced into rings
1 c scallops
1½ c rice, well washed and drained
2 c chicken stock

Preheat oven to 200°C. Heat the oil in a large frying pan. Add onion, capsicum, garlic and chicken and stir fry over a moderate heat for 3 minutes. Add tomatoes, artichoke hearts and peas, cook for 2 minutes, and add the seafood. Stir well, add the rice and stir again. Add the stock and boil. Cover tightly and cook in the oven for 25 minutes. Do not uncover while cooking. Take out of the oven and carefully stir in a knob of butter.

Chicken cannelloni with tomatoes, cream and herbs *(serves 4)*

2 c minced chicken meat
1 medium onion, finely chopped
½ c mixed fresh herbs (dried will not do) — marjoram, oregano, parsley, chervil and garlic are good in any combination or proportion
1 t salt
freshly ground black pepper
1 packet pre-cooked dried cannelloni
50 g butter
1 carrot, peeled and cut into 1-cm dice
1 stick celery, cut into 1-cm dice
1 clove garlic, finely chopped
1 t sugar
6 large tomatoes, skinned, cored, seeded and chopped roughly
1 c cream
½ c Parmesan cheese

Preheat oven to 175°C. Mix chicken, chopped onion and herbs together. Season with salt and pepper. Stuff the cannelloni with this mixture and pack tightly into a deep casserole. Put to one side. Melt the butter in a large frying pan and when it is hot but not brown, add carrot, celery, garlic and sugar. Stir fry over a gentle heat for 3 minutes. Add the tomatoes and boil for 1 minute, then add cream. Taste and season with salt and pepper. Remove from heat and pour over the cannelloni. Sprinkle evenly with Parmesan and bake for 35 minutes.

Roast chicken with bacon and pasta *(serves 4)*

1 medium-sized chicken, roasted with salt, pepper and garlic.
Retain juices in roasting pan.
500 g dried pasta
large knob of butter
½ c diced bacon
1 onion, chopped
2 T fresh marjoram
juice ½ lemon
1 t flour
1 c dry white wine
2 c chicken stock (dried can be used)
grated Parmesan cheese
chopped parsley

Take chicken meat off the bones and set to one side. Cook pasta and keep it hot.

Remove any fat from roasting pan and put it on the heat. To the remaining juices, add butter, bacon, chopped onion and marjoram, and stir fry for 3 minutes until the onion is golden. Scrape the pan as you stir to get any caramelized juices. Add lemon juice and flour. Stir well so the flour is evenly distributed. Add white wine and chicken stock. When the gravy has thickened to the consistency of cream, taste and season with salt and pepper. Put the hot pasta on a serving dish and put the meat on top. Pour on the gravy and sprinkle grated Parmesan and chopped parsley over everything. Serve immediately. If the gravy becomes too thick, thin with more stock.

Chicken with rigatoni, tomatoes and chilli

(photograph opposite p.48) **(serves 4)**

Rigatoni is a dried tubular ridged pasta imported from Italy and available from good grocers.

4 c rigatoni
50 ml olive oil
1 large onion, thinly sliced
2 cloves garlic, chopped
2 dried chillies, finely chopped or pounded in a mortar
2 T chopped fresh coriander (not dried)
1 t sugar
100 g pinenuts
2 c thinly sliced raw chicken breast
50 ml red wine
1 c whole peeled tomatoes in juice (canned), mashed with a fork
1 c chicken stock
grated Parmesan cheese

Cook rigatoni in salted boiling water until "al dente". Put to one side.

In a large frying pan, heat the oil until it is hot but not smoking. Add onion, garlic, chilli, coriander and sugar. Stir fry for 3 minutes over a moderate heat until the onion is golden. Add pinenuts and chicken and cook for a further 3 minutes, stirring constantly. Add the wine and boil for 1 minute, then add tomatoes and stock. Simmer until the chicken is completely cooked. Taste and season with salt and pepper. The sauce should be quite thin.

Add the rigatoni and stir carefully until everything is amalgamated and the pasta is hot. Serve sprinkled with Parmesan cheese.

Judith's warm chicken with penne and asparagus **(serves 4–6)**

Penne is a short tubular Italian dried pasta available from good grocers.

1½-kg boiling fowl, simmered for 2 hours in enough water to cover it, with 1 stalk celery, carrot, onion, peppercorns and a bunch of parsley
4 c dried penne
500 g cooked asparagus
1½ c fresh mayonnaise (p.19)

When cool enough to handle, remove chicken meat from bones, discarding skin and bones. Cook the penne in salted boiling water until it is "al dente", strain, and add to the chicken meat in a large shallow warmed bowl. Add the asparagus and the mayonnaise. Give everything a good stir and serve immediately while it is still warm.

Fried chicken breasts with spaghetti and pesto *(serves 4)*

Pesto is the famous Italian basil sauce; it should be thick, creamy and vivid green.

Pesto

1 large bunch fresh basil
2 cloves garlic
25 g pinenuts
25 g grated Parmesan cheese
100 ml olive oil

Blend the first four ingredients to a paste. With the blender still running, add the olive oil, drop by drop, as for mayonnaise (p.19). Season to taste with salt and pepper. Set to one side.

500 g spaghetti
50 g butter
flour for dusting
4 boneless chicken breasts (halves), boned and skinned
grated Parmesan cheese
chopped parsley
1 c pesto
chopped fresh tomatoes
chopped parsley

Cook the spaghetti in boiling salted water until "al dente", and keep hot. In a large frying pan, melt the butter until it is hot but not brown. Flour the chicken breasts and gently fry them until they are cooked and golden. Dust the hot spaghetti generously with Parmesan cheese and chopped parsley, and make a bed of it on a warm serving dish. Place the chicken on top and spoon the pesto over everything. Garnish with chopped fresh tomatoes and more chopped parsley.

Chicken breast with linguine, tarragon and cream *(serves 4)*

500 g fresh linguine
50 g butter
1 onion, finely chopped
2 T chopped fresh tarragon
2 cloves garlic, finely chopped
2 T chopped parsley
1 T green peppercorns
2 c boneless raw chicken breast, skinned and thinly sliced
100 ml dry white wine
100 ml chicken stock
1 c cream
juice ½ lemon
1 c diced mozzarella cheese

Cook linguine in salted boiling water until "al dente".

In a large frying pan, melt the butter. Add onion, tarragon, garlic, parsley and peppercorns and stir fry gently, without browning, until the onion is golden. Add chicken, stir well, and cook for 3 minutes. Add wine and boil for 1 minute, then add stock and boil for 2 minutes. Finally, add the cream and stir well. Add the linguine and simmer until the pasta is heated through. Taste and season with salt, pepper and lemon juice. Carefully stir in the mozzarella and serve immediately.

Stuffed steamed chicken breasts wrapped in lettuce with fresh noodles *(serves 4)*

2 whole boneless raw chicken breasts, skinned
50 g butter
4 large lettuce leaves
orange peel, parsley, fresh marjoram, thyme
500 g fresh noodles

Stuffing

1 c cooked wild, brown or Thai rice
2 tomatoes, peeled, seeded and chopped
½ c soft wholemeal breadcrumbs
½ c grated sweet apple
large pinch thyme and marjoram (dried)
salt and pepper
1 egg yolk

Cut the chicken breasts down the middle to give 4 large fillets. Gently beat them flat so they increase in size by half and are about 1–2 cm thick. Heat the butter in a large frying pan and sear the breasts over a high heat for 30 seconds each side. Put to one side. Blanch lettuce leaves in boiling water for 20 seconds, cool in iced water and pat dry.

Combine all stuffing ingredients. Divide mixture into 4 and put on one half of each chicken fillet. Fold over. Wrap a lettuce leave around each. Put in a steamer basket over bubbling water with several pieces of orange peel, parsley, fresh marjoram and thyme in it. Cover tightly and steam for 30 minutes.

Serve with fresh noodles, with a generous knob of butter stirred through them.

Sandra's "bits" of chicken with buttered noodles *(serves 4)*

"Bits" of chicken means anything from sliced, boned, skinned breasts to the meat sliced off the legs.

100 g butter
2 c chicken bits, bite-sized
1 T fresh chopped thyme
1 T green peppercorns
½ c diced smoked bacon
½ c rosé wine

Heat half the butter in a large frying pan until hot. Add all the ingredients, except the wine, and stir fry over a high heat until the chicken is cooked; about 5 minutes. Add wine and boil for one minute. Serve over freshly boiled noodles that have the remaining 50 g butter stirred through them.

Chicken with broccoli and anchovies on pasta *(serves 4)*

4 cups cooked pasta (any sort)
50 g butter
1 small onion, finely chopped
10 anchovy fillets, chopped
2 c boneless chicken breast, skinned and thinly sliced
2 T chopped parsley
100 ml dry vermouth
2 c broccoli tips, blanched
½ c cream
grated Parmesan cheese
chopped tomatoes

Cook the pasta in boiling salted water until "al dente", strain and keep hot. In a large frying pan melt the butter. Add onion, anchovies, chicken and parsley. Cook over a high heat, browning slightly until the chicken is cooked. Add the vermouth and boil until the liquid is reduced by half.

Put warm pasta into a warmed shallow bowl. Add the broccoli. Add the cream to the chicken mixture and, when it is boiling, pour everything over the pasta and broccoli. Stir well and sprinkle liberally with Parmesan cheese. Serve immediately with a few cored and chopped tomatoes.

Chicken livers baked with rice *(serves 4)*

50 ml olive oil
2 onions, peeled and chopped
2 cloves garlic, finely chopped
2 T chopped fresh basil or marjoram
½ c sliced mushrooms
1½ cups chicken livers, cleaned and trimmed
250 g white long-grained rice
3 large tomatoes, peeled, cored, seeded and chopped roughly
300 ml light chicken stock (fresh or dried)
50 ml dry white wine
grated Parmesan cheese
chopped parsley

Preheat oven to 200°C. In a heavy frying pan, heat the oil until it is hot. Add onions, garlic, herbs and mushrooms. Stir fry over a moderate heat until the onion is golden. Add chicken livers and stir well, being careful not to break them. Cook until they have coloured all over. Rinse the uncooked rice in plenty of cold water and drain well. Add to the pan and stir well so the rice is coated with oil. Fry for 1 minute. Add tomatoes and continue stirring. Add stock and wine and bring to the boil, stirring well so the rice does not stick.

Cover with a lid or tinfoil, or preferably both, as this dish steams in the liquid and the steam should not escape. Put into the oven for 30 minutes. Do not under any circumstances lift the lid. After 30 minutes open it up and taste the rice, which should be cooked. All the liquid will have disappeared into the other ingredients.

Stir everything up carefully and dust liberally with Parmesan cheese and chopped parsley. Add a large knob of butter, if desired. Season with salt and pepper and serve in the frying pan or casserole.

Cajun chicken with dirty rice and avocado (serves 4)

This recipe was given to me by D. Thompson, the Catering Manager of Hilton Head Hotel in South Carolina. It was originally used with fish but I modified it for chicken.

1 half chicken breast per person, skinned and gently beaten out to 1-cm thickness
tomato wedges
sliced avocado

Cajun spice mixture

2 T sweet paprika
2½ t salt
1 t onion powder
1 t garlic powder
1 t cayenne pepper
¾ t white pepper
½ t dried thyme
½ t dried oregano

Combine all mixture ingredients and press each piece of chicken well into the mixture so the chicken is thoroughly coated.

Dirty rice

This rice is cooked in the oven, so you need a metal casserole with a lid, or a frying pan and tinfoil.

50 g butter
1 large onion, peeled and finely chopped
3 rashers fat bacon, finely chopped
1 capsicum, cored, seeded and chopped
2 cloves garlic, finely chopped
1 t dried thyme
1 t salt
freshly ground black pepper
1 T chopped parsley
2 c whole peeled tomatoes in juice (canned)
350 g rice — it should be a mixture of different rices, i.e. white, wild or Thai Black (the latter must be parboiled)
350 ml chicken stock (fresh or dried)

Preheat oven to 200°C. In a large frying pan, melt the butter. When it is hot but not brown, add the onion, bacon, capsicum, garlic, thyme, salt, pepper and parsley. Stir fry for 5 minutes on a low heat. Add the tomatoes and boil until all the liquid has been absorbed. Stir well so it does not stick. Add the rice and continue stirring for 2 minutes. Add the stock and bring to the boil. Cover tightly and cook in the oven for 30 minutes. Remove the lid and stir well. (Do not remove the lid during cooking time.) The rice is now ready. Keep it hot.

Heat another large heavy frying pan until it is smoking. Continue heating it for another 5 minutes; it has to be incredibly hot. Put ¼ t butter in the middle of each piece of chicken and slap them down on the hot pan, with no other oil or butter. There will be a lot of smoke — this is as it should be. Cook the chicken like this for 3 minutes on each side. The surface will blacken in true Cajun style.

Serve on a good portion of dirty rice, with melted garlic butter for dipping, tomato wedges and plenty of fresh sliced avocado.

Louisiana chicken pilau *(serves 6)*

1½-kg chicken

Simmer chicken in 8 c water, with a stick of celery, a small onion (peeled and sliced), a chopped carrot, peppercorns, bay leaf and handful of parsley. When it is cooked and cool enough to handle, take the flesh off the bones and set aside. Strain and retain the cooking liquid.

Rice

50 g butter
1 large onion, peeled and chopped
1 green capsicum, cored, seeded and chopped
5 bacon rashers, chopped
2 c canned okra, drained
4 large tomatoes, peeled, cored and seeded
350 g best white rice, well washed and drained
50 ml dry white wine
chopped parsley

Preheat oven to 200°C. Melt the butter in a casserole with a lid, or a large frying pan. Add onion, capsicum and bacon, and stir fry over a moderate heat for 5 minutes. Add the okra, tomatoes and rice, and stir well. Add wine and stock from the chicken and bring to the boil. Cover with lid, or tinfoil, and cook in the oven for 25 minutes. Do not lift the lid whilst cooking. When the rice is almost ready, warm the chicken meat in a little chicken stock. When the rice is cooked, uncover and stir carefully so the okra does not break up too much. Arrange the hot chicken on top and sprinkle with chopped parsley. Serve in the pan.

Brown rice, tofu and chicken wings *(serves 4)*

50 ml soya bean oil
¼ c thinly sliced, peeled and chopped root ginger
3 cloves garlic, sliced
16 chicken wings
50 ml water
20 ml soy sauce
2 c cooked brown rice
½ c chopped spring onions
1 c mung bean sprouts
10 x 6-cm block of tofu, cut into 3-cm cubes
tomato wedges

Heat the oil in a wok or deep saucepan until it is hot but not smoking. Add the ginger, garlic and chicken wings. Stir fry for 3 minutes. Add water and soy sauce. Put a lid on the wok and cook over a moderate heat for 10 minutes. Remove the lid and add the rice, spring onions, bean sprouts and tofu, and carefully stir until everything is heated through. If it gets too dry, add a little more water. Season with a little salt and ground black pepper. Garnish with tomato wedges and serve.

Chicken biryani — Indian spiced rice and chicken *(serves 4)*

50 g ghee or butter
1 clove garlic, finely chopped
2 t ground cumin
1 t garam marsala
1 t ground coriander
½ t cayenne pepper (optional)
1 t finely chopped ginger
½ t turmeric
1 t salt
juice ½ lemon
2 large onions, chopped
¼ c currants
¼ c sultanas
1 whole large boneless chicken breast, skinned and sliced into 2-cm thick slices
½ c chopped almonds
350 g Basmati rice soaked in plenty of cold water for 1 hour and well washed
300 ml water or chicken stock

Preheat oven to 200°C. In a large metal casserole or large frying pan (which can be covered in tinfoil), melt the butter or ghee until hot but not smoking. Add garlic, cumin, garam marsala, coriander, cayenne, ginger, turmeric and salt. Stir fry the spices for 1 minute, then add lemon juice, onions, currants, sultanas and chicken. Fry over a low heat for 3 minutes and stir well so everything is covered with the spices. Add almonds, rice and the water or stock, and bring to the boil. Cover tightly and cook in the oven for 25–30 minutes. Do not uncover while cooking. When it is cooked, stir everything up so all the ingredients are evenly distributed. Serve with the following:

Cucumber and apple raita

½ telegraph cucumber, with skin on, grated and squeezed dry
1 eating apple, grated, with skin on
½ t ground cumin
¼ t salt
freshly ground black pepper
1½ c plain yoghurt
juice ½ lemon
1 T chopped fresh mint leaves

Combine all ingredients well and serve separately.

Chicken lasagne *(serves 4)*

This is a traditional lasagne in its make-up but the tedium of the lasagne method, with all its different operations, is honed down to the bare essentials, giving an incredibly fresh look, taste and lightness to the dish. Unorthodox, but delicious.

First, the meat

50 g butter
1 large onion, finely chopped
2 cloves garlic, finely chopped
3 boneless chicken breasts (halves), skinned and finely sliced

In a large frying pan, heat the butter until it is hot but not brown. Add onion, garlic and chicken, and stir fry for 3 minutes, until the onion is golden but not browned. Remove from heat and set aside.

Tomato sauce

50 ml olive oil
8 large fresh tomatoes, skinned, cored and roughly chopped
½ c chopped fresh basil

Heat the oil until just smoking, add tomatoes and cook for 1 minute, then add basil and season with salt and pepper. Take off the heat immediately and set to one side.

Also have ready

1½ c fresh ricotta cheese
2 c cooked chopped spinach
2–3 large sheets precooked lasagne
1 c diced mozzarella

Preheat oven to 175°C. In a deep casserole dish, about 20 cm in diameter and 10 cm deep, place a thin layer of chicken mixture. Cover with a layer of tomatoes, then a layer of ricotta, then spinach and then lasagne. Repeat until each is used up. Top with mozzarella. Bake for 30–35 minutes. Serve with plain green salad.

Pies, Terrines and Pâtés

Alexalensia's chicken terrine

Make the day before you intend eating it.

3 chickens, about 1 kg each
1 t salt
juice ½ lemon
50 ml white wine
pinch mace
3 T chopped tarragon
500 g pork pieces
1 egg
1 c fresh breadcrumbs
1 T chopped parsley
2 shallots, finely chopped
500 g streaky bacon rashers
bay leaves

Bone the chickens, discarding skin and bones. Cut breasts into thin strips and put into an earthenware bowl with salt, lemon juice, white wine, mace and 2 t chopped tarragon. Marinate for 3–4 hours. Mince the rest of the chicken and the pork, and mix with egg, breadcrumbs, parsley, shallots and the remainder of the tarragon. Set aside.

Line a large terrine dish with bacon, keeping some for the top. Put in a layer of minced meat, then a layer of sliced chicken. Continue in layers, finishing with mince, then cover with bacon. Place a line of bay leaves on top and cover tightly (tinfoil will do). Cook in a water bath at 160°C for 1¾ hours. Put a light weight on the terrine while cooling. Refrigerate overnight. Slice thinly the next day.

R.K's chicken liver pâté

500 g chicken livers, cleaned and trimmed
3 T brandy
50 g butter
2 small onions, finely chopped
4 rashers bacon, rind removed and chopped
½ t dried thyme
1 bay leaf
3 T dry sherry
¼ c cream
2 T chopped parsley
clarified butter

Chop the chicken livers and place in a basin with the brandy. Marinate 1½ hours, then drain, reserving the brandy. In a heavy frying pan, melt half the butter until it is hot but not brown. Add livers and sauté until they are browned. Remove from the pan and set aside. Melt the remaining butter, add onions, bacon, thyme and bay leaf. Brown them over a moderate heat for 5 minutes. Add livers and continue stir frying for a further 4–5 minutes. Remove the bay leaf, add the brandy, sherry, cream and parsley, and season well with salt and pepper. Take off the heat and blend the mixture until it is smooth, or push through a fine sieve. Put the pâté into an earthenware dish and pour on a thin layer of clarified butter. Refrigerate. Use the next day if possible.

Cracked pepper pâté

Basic R.K.'s pâté (p.38), but instead of pouring on clarified butter at the end, sprinkle on a 1-cm thick layer of cracked black peppercorns.

Green peppercorn pâté

Basic R.K.'s pâté (p.38), but after the pâté has been blended, thoroughly stir in 1½ T of green peppercorns. Pour on clarified butter.

Hazelnut pâté

Basic R.K.'s pâté (p.38), but add ½ c roughly chopped roasted hazelnuts with the bacon and onion, and then brown.

Lemon and coriander pâté

Basic R.K.'s pâté (p.38), but add juice and rind of 1 lemon and 1 T chopped coriander with the bacon and onion.

Duck liver pâté with prunes

Substitute duck livers for chicken, or use a mixture of both as in R.K.'s basic recipe (p.38), and marinate the livers in 3 T port as well as brandy. When adding bacon and onions, also add grated rind of an orange, 8 finely chopped pitted prunes and the juice of ½ lemon. Continue as instructed but do not blend the pâté too smooth. Leave it quite coarse and finish with clarified butter as usual.

Cream cheese and turkey pâté

A good way of using up leftover turkey or chicken.

1 c chopped cooked turkey or chicken meat
1 c cream cheese
½ c cream
juice 1 lemon
2 cloves garlic, chopped
2 T chopped parsley
1 T chopped fresh coriander
1 T green peppercorns

Put first 6 ingredients into a food processor, and process until smooth. Taste and season well with salt and pepper. Stir in the green peppercorns so they are evenly distributed. Push into a container, cover and refrigerate.

Crumbed chicken livers

A great hors d'oeuvre.

As many chicken livers as you need, cleaned and trimmed, and the two lobes separated

Dust each piece in the seasoned flour and then dip into a mixture of egg beaten with milk. Coat well with breadcrumbs. Fry in oil over a moderate heat until golden brown and just pink inside. Drain well on paper towels and allow to go cold. Serve on crisp lettuce leaves with plenty of lemon wedges to squeeze over them.

Chicken and pork rillettes

Rillettes are a soft pork pâté that is made by "melting" fat pork on a low heat for several hours. The taste and texture are superb. The addition of chicken meat gives a smoother result.

1 kg fat belly pork, skinned and cut into 2-cm cubes
200 g diced pork fat
500 g boneless skinned chicken meat, cut into 2-cm cubes
4 cloves garlic, finely chopped

Place a heavy-based saucepan over a gentle heat. Add all the ingredients and season well. Let the meat get hot, stirring frequently so it does not stick. When it is hot and the pork fat is translucent, cover with cold water. Cook the meat so it is barely simmering until the fat has completely disappeared and everything is a gelatinous mush. It could take up to 4 or 5 hours, but it's worth it.

Gently break up any lumps by slowly turning a hand beater through it. Pour into an earthenware container and refrigerate. It will set into a spreadable pâté. At no stage during cooking should it become dry. If it does, add more water. However, all the water must have gone by the time it is cooked.

Serve with warm, freshly cooked beetroot cut into cubes and dressed with vinaigrette (p.17) and chopped parsley.

Ballotine of duck with pistachios and prunes

A very elegant dish as a first course for a dinner party.

2-kg duck, boned
50 ml port or Madeira
500 g minced fat belly pork
1 duck liver, finely chopped
1 small onion, finely chopped
juice and rind 1 orange
1 t salt
½ t thyme
freshly ground black pepper
1 t sugar
tiny pinch saltpetre (optional) to keep the pork pink
25 ml brandy
pinch mace and nutmeg
100 g shelled whole pistachios
10 pitted prunes
bay leaves

Marinate the duck in the port for 2–3 hours. Mix pork, liver, onion, orange, salt, thyme, pepper, sugar, saltpetre, brandy, spices and pistachios together and set aside for 2–3 hours.

Drain the duck and add the liquid to the pork mix. Line a long narrow terrine dish — a loaf tin will do — with the duck, along the bottom and up the sides, with plenty overhanging to use for covering the top. Put in half the pork mix and arrange a line of prunes down the middle. Put in the rest of the pork mix and fold the duck over the top. You now have a long duck sausage, stuffed with pork mix. Do not use a tin that is too big. The ballotine should completely fill it. Put a line of bayleaves along the top and cover tightly with foil. Bake in a water bath at 160°C for 1½–1¾ hours. Press with a light weight as it cools.

Use the next day, sliced. Excellent served with an orange and lettuce salad.

Chicken liver quenelles — souffléed chicken liver dumplings (serves 4)

chicken stock for poaching
125 g chicken livers, cleaned and trimmed
1 shallot, minced
1 egg white

Heat the stock until it is just simmering. Put the livers, shallot and egg white into the food processor or blender. Season with salt and pepper, and process until smooth. Using 2 teaspoons, take a little of the liver mixture, shape it into an oval, and carefully drop it into the simmering stock. Do not let it boil. Poach for one minute on each side, then remove and drain on paper towels. Keep hot. Serve as an entrée with Béarnaise sauce or a thin, fresh tomato sauce.

Chicken and kumara pie ***(serves 4 with salad)***

25 g butter
1 large onion, thinly sliced
2 rashers bacon, rind removed and chopped
2 c chopped raw chicken breast
1 large kumara, cooked and chopped into 3-cm dice
2 T chopped parsley
1 T flour
25 ml dry white wine
1 c chicken stock
½ c cream
enough puff or flaky pastry to cover your pie dish
beaten egg

Preheat oven to 200°C. In a large frying pan, melt the butter, then add onion and bacon. Stir fry over a moderate heat for 3 minutes without browning. Add the chicken and cook for 2 minutes. Add kumara and parsley. Sprinkle on the flour and stir everything carefully. Add wine and stock, and stir slowly, making sure the flour does not go lumpy. Add cream and boil for 1 minute. Taste and season with salt and pepper. Cool. Pour into a pie dish, roll out the pastry and cover the pie. Make one or two slashes in the top to let the steam escape and decorate with the off-cuts of pastry. Brush with beaten egg and rest for 10 minutes. Bake until the pastry if puffed and golden; about 20–25 minutes.

Greek spinach, chicken and feta pie *(photograph opposite p.49)* ***(serves 6)***

A variation of the traditional Greek Spanakopitta.

10 sheets filo pastry
butter, melted
1 whole boneless raw chicken breast, skinned and finely sliced
2 T chopped fresh dill
2 T chopped parsley
1 c chopped spring onions
1 kg spinach, well washed, leaves blanched for 1 minute in boiling water, refreshed in cold water, and well dried on paper towels
2 eggs, beaten
100 g feta cheese, crumbled

Preheat oven to 180°C. Line a pie dish with 5 leaves of filo pastry, brushing melted butter between each. Set to one side. Put a damp cloth over the remaining 5 sheets so they do not dry out. Melt a little butter in a pan and quickly stir fry the chicken, dill, parsley and spring onions over a moderate heat for 3 minutes. Cool. Season well with freshly ground black pepper and a little salt (the feta cheese is salty). Roughly chop the spinach and spread it over the filo in the dish. Mix the eggs, cheese and chicken mixture together and spread it over the spinach. Top with the remaining 5 sheets of filo, with melted butter between each. I do not bother to trim the pastry as the frilly edge looks attractive.

Brush the top with melted butter and bake for 40 minutes. Serve hot or cool.

Creamed chicken, oyster and parsley pie

1 T butter
1 onion, finely chopped
½ cup chopped celery
2 c sliced chicken breast, skinned
25 ml dry white wine
juice ½ lemon
12 oysters, roughly chopped, and their liquor
1½ T flour
about ½ c chicken stock
1 c cream
½ c chopped parsley
flakey pastry to cover the pie dish

Preheat oven to 200°C. Melt the butter in a large frying pan. Add onion and celery and stir fry over moderate heat for 2 minutes until the onion is golden but not browned. Add the chicken and fry for 2 minutes. Add wine, lemon juice and oyster liquor. Sprinkle in the flour and stir well. Pour in stock and stir well again, then add cream. Bring to the boil and continue stirring to avoid lumps of flour. Add oysters and parsley. Remove from heat and cool. Pour into a pie dish. (If the mixture becomes too thick, thin with chicken stock or cream.)

Roll out the pastry 1 cm thick and make a lid for the pie. Brush the top with beaten egg and make 2 or 3 slashes in the pastry to let the steam escape. Rest in a cool place for 10 minutes before baking for 20 minutes or until the pastry is puffed and golden.

Chicken tamale pie ***(serves 6)***

An American "pie" that is a spicy chicken stew surrounded by cornmeal dough (like Italian Polenta) and baked in the oven. It is very filling!

Filling

50 g butter
2 onions, finely sliced
1 clove garlic, chopped
10 black olives, stoned
2 T fresh coriander
½ t cayenne pepper
1 t sugar
3 c chopped raw chicken meat, skinned
salt and pepper
2 c whole peeled tomatoes in juice (canned)

Melt the butter in a heavy frying pan. Add onions, garlic, olives, coriander, cayenne and sugar. Stir fry without browning for 4 minutes. Add chicken and season well with salt and pepper. Stir fry for 4 minutes. Add tomatoes and break them up with a fork. Bring to the boil and simmer until everything has reduced to a thick stew. Take off the heat and set aside.

Dough

5 c chicken stock
2 c fine cornmeal

Bring the stock to the boil in a large saucepan and sprinkle in the cornmeal, stirring continuously. The stock will thicken to a sticky mush. Cook over a gentle heat for 5 minutes but do not let it burn. When a spoon will stand up in it unsupported, take it off the heat. Cool and then line the bottom and sides of a well-buttered ovenproof dish with half the dough. Pour in the chicken stew and cover with the rest of the dough. Bake for 1¼ hours at 140°C.

Casseroles and Stews

Gulam Rasool's Kashmiri chicken

(photograph opposite p.64) ***(serves 4)***

This dish, like most Kashmiri dishes, is hot, but you can adjust the chilli to your own taste. I ate it on a houseboat on the Dal Lake in Kashmir, Northern India. Delicious!

50 g butter or ghee
1 t chopped fresh ginger
1 t garam marsala
½ t cayenne pepper or 1 small fresh chilli, finely chopped
1 t ground cumin
1 t salt
1 t sugar
1 small onion, finely chopped
juice 1 lemon
1.5-kg chicken, cut into 6 pieces (wings, legs and 2 half breasts), backbone discarded
3 c whole peeled tomatoes in juice (canned), mashed
2 large bunches spinach, well washed with leaves removed from stems

In a heavy saucepan, melt the butter until it is hot but not burning. Add the spices, salt and sugar. Stir fry over a moderate heat for 1 minute. Add onion and lemon juice and stir over a lower heat for 2 minutes. Add chicken and turn so that it is well coated in the onion and spice mixture. Add tomatoes and spinach, and stir well. Cover with a lid or tinfoil and simmer for 20–25 minutes until the chicken is tender. Add a little water if the mixture gets too dry. Serve with plain boiled rice and yoghurt.

Cinnamon chicken ***(serves 4)***

4 chicken breasts (halves), skinned, do not discard skin
1 T coconut oil
2 T brown sugar
2 onions, finely chopped
½ green capsicum, cut into fine strips
3 cloves garlic, finely chopped
1 t ground cinnamon
4 large tomatoes, skinned, cored and seeded
½ c sultanas
½ c chicken stock

Fry the chicken skins in a heavy pan. When they begin to sizzle, add coconut oil and breasts and stir fry without burning for 10 minutes. Discard the skins and sprinkle brown sugar over the chicken. Turn it constantly so that the sugar does not burn. Add onions, capsicum and garlic, and stir fry for 2 minutes. Add cinnamon and roughly chopped tomatoes. Simmer on a very low heat for 10 minutes. Add sultanas and a little chicken stock so that the sauce is quite runny. Simmer for 15 minutes, adding more stock if the sauce becomes too thick. Taste and season with salt and pepper. Serve with plain steamed rice with a pinch of saffron added.

Grant's chicken vindaloo *(serves 6)*

1 c ghee or clarified butter
2 large onions, sliced
2 green chillies, finely chopped
1½ T chopped fresh ginger
3 cloves garlic, chopped
1½ t turmeric
1 t ground coriander
1 t garam marsala
1.5-kg chicken, jointed and skinned
3 T vinegar
1¼ c water
⅔ c shredded coconut
1 t salt
chopped cucumber

Heat the ghee until it is hot but not smoking, and stir fry the onions and chillies until the onion is golden. Add ginger, garlic, turmeric, coriander and garam marsala. Stir fry for 23 minutes, but do not let the spices burn. Add chicken pieces, turning them over so they are covered with the onion and spice mixture. Add vinegar and water. Cover and simmer for 25–30 minutes. When the chicken is just cooked, remove the lid and boil rapidly until the sauce thickens. Add coconut and salt, and simmer for a further 10 minutes. As a separate dish, serve half a finely chopped cucumber mixed with a cup of plain yoghurt, and plenty of plain boiled rice.

Spiced chicken with mango *(serves 4)*

2 T coconut oil
1 T butter
½ t ground cinnamon
½ T ground cloves
½ T ginger, finely chopped
½ t ground nutmeg
2 cloves garlic, finely chopped
2 green chillies, finely chopped
1 large onion
½ c sultanas
3 c diced chicken meat (breast, leg, whatever)
1 c chicken stock
2 mangoes, peeled and sliced

Heat the oil and butter in a heavy frying pan. When it is hot, add the cinnamon, cloves, ginger and nutmeg. Stir fry without burning for 1 minute. Add garlic, chillies, onion and sultanas, and stir fry gently until the onion is golden brown. Add chicken meat and brown carefully, stirring constantly. Reduce the heat to low and moisten the mixture with about 1 c of chicken stock. Simmer for 10 minutes, adding more stock to keep the mixture wet. Add half the mango slices and simmer for another 10 minutes, adding more stock if necessary. Taste and season with salt and pepper. Just before the 10 minutes is up, add the remaining mango slices and heat them through. Serve with saffron rice or dirty rice (p.34).

Chicken and potato curry *(serves 6)*

½ c ghee or clarified butter
¼ t cayenne pepper
2 t ground cumin
1 t turmeric
1 t black mustard seeds
1 t chopped fresh ginger
2 cloves garlic, finely chopped
juice ½ lemon
2 onions, chopped
4 boneless chicken breasts (halves), skinned and chopped
6 small parboiled potatoes, skin on, sliced thickly
4 large tomatoes, skinned, cored, seeded and sliced roughly
½ c fresh coriander

Heat the ghee in a large frying pan until it is hot but not smoking. Add spices and garlic (but not coriander). Stir fry for 1 minute, then add lemon juice and onion. Stir fry for 3 minutes or until the onion is golden. Add chicken and potatoes, and give everything a good stir so that the spice mixture is evenly distributed. Add the tomatoes, fresh coriander and enough water to just cover everything. Bring to the boil, stirring continuously, and simmer for 30 minutes. Taste and season with salt and pepper. Serve with plain rice and a side dish of bananas sliced and mixed with lemon juice and coconut.

Lemon chicken with chick peas and spinach *(serves 6)*

4 T olive oil
2 onions, finely chopped
4 cloves garlic, finely chopped
1½ t turmeric
rind of 1 lemon
1 stick celery, cut in 1-cm dice
1 carrot, cut in 1-cm dice
¼ t cayenne pepper
2-kg roasting fowl, jointed
200 g chick peas, soaked overnight in plenty of cold water
juice 2 lemons
2 c chopped spinach leaves
700 ml water

In a heavy deep saucepan, heat the oil and when it is hot add onions, garlic, turmeric, lemon rind, celery, carrot and cayenne. Stir fry for 3–4 minutes until the onion is golden but not brown. Add chicken and stir fry until it is coated with the turmeric mixture. Add the drained chick peas and stir well. Add lemon juice, spinach and water, and cover. Simmer for 1½ hours until the chicken is tender and the liquid has reduced a little. Taste and season with salt and pepper.

Turkey breast baked with Parmesan and mushrooms *(serves 4–6)*

This dish is very rich. It is a variation on a classic northern Italian dish that calls for white truffles. However, mushrooms, though not as grand, are delicious.

½ raw turkey breast, skinned, boned and sliced thinly; flatten each slice with a mallet so they are about the same thickness
seasoned flour
100 g butter
¼ c finely sliced prosciutto (Italian ham)
1½ c thinly sliced, well washed mushrooms
75 ml dry white wine
500 ml stock made from the turkey carcass (see chicken stock p.7) or 500 ml good chicken stock
1½ c freshly grated Parmesan cheese

Preheat oven to 200°C. Dust the turkey slices in seasoned flour. Melt the butter in a large frying pan and when it is hot, fry the turkey slices quickly for 30 seconds each side. Do not let the butter burn. When the turkey slices are cooked, layer them in a large shallow ovenproof dish and sprinkle on the ham. Keep the heat in the frying pan moderate and stir fry the mushrooms for 2 minutes, add the wine, bring to the boil and pour over the turkey and ham. Spread the mushrooms evenly over the turkey and pour in enough stock to just cover. Sprinkle the cheese evenly over everything and bake for 15–20 minutes or until the cheese has melted and a rich buttery sauce has formed.

Poulet a la creme d'estragon — Tarragon cream chicken *(serves 4)*

Simple, elegant and very good.

50 g butter
1.5-kg chicken cut into 4 pieces
1 T finely chopped fresh tarragon (not dried)
50 ml dry white wine
100 ml well-flavoured chicken stock
200 ml cream
salt and freshly ground pepper
2 sprigs extra tarragon

Melt the butter in a heavy frying pan. When it is hot, add the chicken and cook until golden brown on each side. Add tarragon and wine, and bring to the boil. Add stock and simmer for 25 minutes. When chicken is cooked, remove from pan and keep it hot on a serving dish. Add the cream to the pan and boil until it reduces and is thick enough to coast the spoon. Taste and season with salt and pepper. Pour over the chicken in the dish. Garnish with whole tarragon leaves.

Chicken with rigatoni, tomatoes and chilli (p.30)

La poule au pot — chicken poached with vegetables *(serves 6)*

Stuffing

1 chicken liver, finely chopped
100 g minced belly pork or good sausage meat
1 clove garlic, finely chopped
2 T chopped parsley
1 c fresh breadcrumbs soaked in milk or water and squeezed dry

50 g butter
2-kg chicken
6 small onions, peeled
1 small turnip, peeled and quartered
2 carrots, peeled and thickly sliced
12 mushrooms
2 sticks celery, sliced
1 leek, peeled and sliced
2 bay leaves
sprig parsley
100 ml dry white wine

Combine all the stuffing ingredients and stuff the chicken. Sew or skewer the cavity closed.

In a deep saucepan, melt the butter and when it is hot, add the stuffed chicken and brown all over without burning. Add vegetables, herbs and wine, and cover everything with boiling water. Simmer gently for 1½–2 hours, skimming off any scum. Half an hour before the chicken is ready, you can replace the vegetables with new ones if you like, although I prefer the originals. When it is ready, remove the bird and carve in the usual way. Serve the vegetables around it. The broth can be served as a first course soup, maybe with some pasta or rice cooked in it, or alternatively you can thicken some of it and use it like gravy with the chicken. Do not waste it as it will freeze well and is a superior chicken stock.

I sometimes cook quite a lot of potatoes in with the chicken, adding them 30 minutes before serving. They thicken the broth and you have a "one pot" meal, which is very convenient. If I add potatoes, I serve the meal in large flat soup plates with plenty of liquid so that it is like a very hearty stew.

Greek spinach, chicken and feta pie (p.42)

Coq au vin rouge *(serves 4)*

An underrated and neglected dish. Worth making, provided the chicken is not cooked to rags!

600 ml good red wine
150 ml well flavoured chicken stock (preferably homemade)
50 g butter
½ c bacon, cut into 1-cm dice
12 little pickling onions
1.5-kg roasting fowl, cut into 4 pieces
25 ml brandy
1½ c small button mushrooms, well washed
1 T butter mixed well with
1 T flour

Boil wine and stock in a saucepan until the volume has reduced by half. Set aside.

Melt the 50 g butter in a wide heavy saucepan, add the bacon and stir fry for 1 minute — do not let the butter burn. Add onions and stir fry until they are golden, then add the chicken and do the same. Pour in the brandy, let it bubble and light it. Shake the pan and, when the flames have subsided, add the wine-stock mixture. Simmer for 40 minutes, until the chicken is tender. Add mushrooms 15 minutes before the chicken is ready. Do not overcook the chicken.

Remove the chicken, bacon and vegetables from the saucepan and arrange on a serving dish. Bring the cooking liquid to the boil, crumble in the mixed flour and butter, and whisk continuously. Bring back to the boil and boil for 1 minute (the butter-flour mixture will have thickened the sauce). Taste and season with salt and pepper. Pour over the chicken and serve with thin rounds of French bread painted with olive oil and dried golden brown in the oven.

Chicken braised with red cabbage *(serves 4)*

50 ml olive oil
1 onion, finely sliced
1 clove garlic, chopped
1 T fresh thyme leaves
1 T chopped parsley
2 rashers bacon, chopped
1 t sugar
1.5-kg roasting chicken, cut into 4 pieces
1 large apple, skin on, cored and sliced
1 small red cabbage, cored and finely shredded
50 ml red wine
1 T vinegar
100 ml chicken stock

Heat the olive oil over a moderate heat in a deep heavy saucepan with a close fitting lid. Add onion, garlic, thyme, parsley, bacon and sugar, and season well with salt and pepper. Stir fry over a gentle heat until the onion is transparent but not browned. Add chicken pieces and continue cooking, increasing the heat a little so they just brown. Add apple and cabbage, and stir well. Add wine, vinegar and stock, cover the pan tightly, and turn the heat down. Cook for 45 minutes, turning the chicken occasionally. The cabbage will reduce to a thick sauce.

Braised chicken with pork, mushroom and olive stuffing *(serves 4)*

Stuffing

1 T soft butter
1 chicken liver, chopped
1 chicken heart, chopped
2 T chopped bacon
2 T chopped salami
100 g diced belly pork
2 cloves garlic, chopped
¼ c sliced mushrooms
100 g pitted green olives
1 T butter mixed well into
1 T flour

3 T olive oil
1.5-kg chicken
25 ml brandy
600 ml stock

Do not chop stuffing ingredients too finely. Mix them all together and stuff chicken. Sew or skewer the cavity closed.

Preheat oven to 200°C. In a deep casserole with a cover (tinfoil will do), heat the olive oil until it is hot but not smoking, and brown the stuffed chicken carefully until it is golden brown all over. Pour in the brandy and set alight. When the flames have subsided, pour in the stock. The chicken should only be half covered by stock. Cover the casserole and bake for 1 hour, basting frequently.

Remove chicken from casserole and keep hot on carving dish. Skim fat off the cooking liquid and then boil. Crumble butter-flour mixture into the boiling stock, whisking all the time. When the sauce has thickened, serve separately with the chicken.

Chicken breasts with apple, port and pecans *(serves 4)*

25 g butter
4 chicken breasts
seasoned flour
1 small c pecan nuts
juice ½ lemon
50 ml port
50 ml chicken stock
1 apple, cored, peeled and thinly sliced
100 ml cream

Melt the butter in a heavy pan and brown the chicken breasts which have been rolled in the seasoned flour. Add pecan nuts, lemon juice, and season well with salt and pepper. Pour in port and chicken stock. Bring to the boil and simmer until the chicken is cooked, about 15 minutes. Remove chicken from pan and keep hot on a serving dish. Add apple slices and cream to pan and bring to the boil. Reduce by fast boiling until the sauce is thick enough to cover the chicken breasts lightly. (If the sauce gets too thick, thin with a little more stock.) The apple slices will be cooked. Pour over chicken breasts and serve.

Poulet à la creme *(serves 4)*

50 g butter
1 onion, finely chopped
1.5-kg chicken, cut into 4 pieces
300 ml cream
2 beaten egg yolks
juice ½ lemon

Melt the butter in a heavy frying pan over a gentle heat. Add onion and chicken pieces, and braise until the chicken is tender. Pour on the cream and boil until the sauce just thickens. Remove the chicken and keep hot on a serving dish. Mix the beaten egg yolks and lemon juice together. Take the cream mixture off the boil and quickly whisk in the egg yolks. Do not boil again or it will curdle. Taste and season with salt and pepper. Pour over the chicken and serve.

A good variation on this dish is to pour on a few tablespoons of brandy and light it just before adding the cream. Then add 3 peeled, cored and seeded tomatoes (roughly chopped), a handful of button mushrooms and 1 T chopped parsley, with the cream. The taste of cooked fresh tomatoes, cream and chicken is very good.

Chicken cooked in milk *(serves 4)*

75 g butter
1 small onion, finely chopped
2 T chopped ham
2 cloves garlic, finely chopped
1 dessertspoon finely chopped fresh marjoram or basil
1.5-kg chicken
enough milk to cover

Melt the butter in a deep heavy saucepan. Add onion, ham, garlic and herbs. Stir fry over a gentle heat until golden brown. Add the chicken and brown lightly all over. Boil the milk in another pan and pour on enough to cover the chicken. Simmer for 1 hour without stirring, then stir up the brown crust on the top and sides. Carefully simmer for another 30 minutes, making sure the liquid does not evaporate and burn. Taste and season with salt and pepper. When the chicken is cooked, break it up and arrange on a serving dish. Pour on the sauce and eat hot or cold.

Circassian chicken *(serves 4)*

2-kg chicken
2 onions, peeled and thickly sliced
2 carrots, sliced
2 sticks celery, chopped
1 clove garlic, crushed
1 bay leaf
1 large sprig parsley
100 ml white wine
200 g blanched almonds, hazelnuts and walnuts, ground to a powder in a food processor
salt, pepper and lemon juice
1 T paprika mixed with
2 T olive oil

Put the first 8 ingredients into a large saucepan, cover with water and simmer for 1 hour or until the chicken is tender. Remove chicken from saucepan, carve and keep hot on a serving dish. Strain the stock carefully through a fine sieve and put 600 ml into a clean pan. Bring to the boil and stir in nuts. Taste and season with salt, pepper and lemon juice. Pour over the chicken and decorate with dribbles of paprika/olive oil mixture. Serve with plain steamed rice with a generous knob of butter stirred into it at the last minute.

R.K's chicken marengo *(serves 4)*

4 boneless chicken breasts (halves)
50 g seasoned flour
200 g butter
4 rashers bacon, chopped
2 small onions, chopped
1 t sugar
200 g mushrooms, sliced
1 t fresh oregano
4 tomatoes, peeled, cored and chopped
6 T sherry or Madeira
3 c chicken stock

Roll chicken in seasoned flour and brown in 100 g butter in a frying pan over a moderate heat. Put into a casserole. In the same frying pan, melt the remaining butter and cook bacon, onions, sugar, mushrooms and oregano for 2–3 minutes, until the onion is golden brown. Add remaining flour and stir well. Add tomatoes, sherry or Madeira and chicken stock, and bring to the boil. Pour on the chicken and cook in a slow oven for 2 hours. Serve with rice and a salad.

Chicken and banana casserole *(serves 4)*

4 unripe bananas, peeled and thickly sliced
50 g butter
1 onion, chopped
4 rashers bacon, chopped
1 T finely chopped fresh ginger
1 clove garlic, chopped
1.5-kg chicken, jointed
4 tomatoes, peeled, cored and seeded
1 c water or chicken stock

Drop bananas into boiling water and cook until tender. Drain and set aside. Melt butter in a heavy pan. Add onion, bacon, ginger and garlic, and stir fry over a moderate heat until the onion is golden. Add chicken and brown lightly. Add tomatoes and stock. Bring to the boil and simmer for 25 minutes or until the chicken is tender. Add bananas 15 minutes before chicken is ready. Taste and season as necessary. Serve with buttered or dirty rice (p.34)

Yankee chicken and oyster stew *(serves 4)*

100 g butter
1.5-kg chicken, jointed
salt and pepper
1 t chopped fresh sage
½ c milk
2 dozen oysters
1 c cream
1 t chopped fresh basil

Preheat oven to 190°C. Melt the butter in a metal casserole and gently fry the chicken until golden brown. Season well with salt and pepper, then add sage and milk. Cover and bake for 1¼ hours. Add oysters, cream and basil, and bake uncovered for another 15 minutes. Serve in a soup plate with hot scones made with a little cornmeal or wholemeal flour as well as white.

Chicken paprika *(serves 4)*

100 g butter
2 large onions, sliced
2 t paprika
2-kg chicken, jointed
seasoned flour
2 T tomato concentrate
300 ml sour cream

Melt the butter in a heavy frying pan, add onions and paprika, and fry over a gentle heat until golden brown. Roll chicken in seasoned flour and brown. Add tomato concentrate and enough water to just cover the chicken. Stir well. Simmer until the chicken is tender. Add sour cream, bring to the boil and simmer for another 5 minutes. Taste and season with salt and pepper. Serve with hot buttered noodles.

Indonesian chicken *(serves 4)*

50 g butter
1 large onion finely chopped
1 T chopped fresh ginger
2 cloves garlic, chopped
Spices — grind together
 5 red dried chillies,
 5 peppercorns, 4 cloves,
 ½ t turmeric, 4-cm piece
 cinnamon, 1 cardamom pod
2-kg chicken, jointed
seasoned flour
2 T tamarind paste or vinegar
400-ml can coconut cream

Melt the butter in a frying pan over a gentle heat. Add onion, ginger and garlic. Stir fry until browned. Add spices and fry for 1 minute, then add chicken pieces which have been rolled in seasoned flour. Cover and cook gently for 15 minutes. Uncover and add tamarind or vinegar and coconut cream. Stir well. Cover and simmer for 15 minutes. Taste and season with salt and pepper. Serve with rice and separate dishes of bananas sprinkled with lemon juice, and mango chutney.

Pheasant stewed with cream and apples (serves 4)

100 g butter
1 small onion, very finely chopped
1 small carrot, very finely chopped
1 pheasant
50 ml Calvados (french apple brandy) or whiskey
4 sweet apples, peeled, cored and thickly sliced
2 c cream

Preheat oven to 180°C. Melt the butter in a metal casserole. Add onion and carrot and fry gently until the onion is golden brown. Add pheasant and brown on all sides. Pour in Calvados or whiskey and let it bubble. Pack the apple slices around the pheasant (make sure the casserole is not too big, as you need it quite full of everything) and pour on the cream. Cover tightly and bake for 40 minutes or until the bird is tender. You will have a tender, moist pheasant (they can be very dry) with a creamy apple purée surrounding it. Taste the purée and season with salt and pepper. Serve poured over the carved pheasant.

Pheasant stewed with orange, red wine and grapes (serves 4)

Marinade
100 ml red wine
1 t sugar
1 sprig fresh thyme
1 clove garlic, chopped
1 small onion, finely chopped
1 c orange juice
grated rind 1 orange

1 pheasant jointed
butter
seasoned flour
100 ml chicken stock
1 c seeded grapes

Marinate the pheasant overnight in the marinade. Next day, preheat the oven to 200°C). Melt some butter in a metal casserole. Roll the drained pheasant pieces in the seasoned flour and gently fry them until golden brown. Pour on the marinade and stock. Cover the casserole and cook in the oven for 35–40 minutes until the bird is tender. Take the pheasant out of the sauce and arrange it on a serving dish. Keep hot. Add the grapes to the sauce and boil furiously for 3–4 minutes. The sauce will thicken a little but it should be quite thin. If it gets too thick, add a little more stock. Taste and season with salt and pepper. Pour onto the pheasant. Serve with boiled rice.

Spanish pheasant casserole *(serves 4)*

2 T olive oil
1 onion, sliced
½ c chopped raw ham (Italian prosciutto will do)
1 red capsicum, thinly sliced
1 pheasant
4 tomatoes, peeled, cored, seeded and chopped
150 ml red wine
300 ml chicken stock
slices of bread, fried golden in olive oil

Heat olive oil in a metal casserole. Add onion, ham and capsicum and stir fry for 2–3 minutes, then add the pheasant. Brown, then add tomatoes, wine and stock. Simmer gently until the pheasant is cooked, remove pieces from casserole and put on the fried bread.

Bring the sauce to the boil and let it thicken by reducing (it should be the consistency of cream). Taste and season with salt and pepper. Pour onto the pheasant. Serve with rice.

Braised duck with mushrooms and olives (serves 4)

Ducks are usually very fatty and the fat has a strong flavour. The initial roasting is important when braising or stewing duck, as it removes a lot of the fat so that it does not overpower the sauce. Ducks do not have a lot of meat, so this is just enough for 4.

2-kg duck
salt and pepper
2 T olive oil
1 small onion, finely sliced
2 cloves garlic
½ t ground black pepper
1 large sprig thyme
1 t sugar
100 ml port or Madeira
500 ml chicken stock
juice ½ lemon
2 c sliced mushrooms
1 c pitted green olives
1 T cornflour

Prick the duck all over so the fat can escape easily. Sprinkle with salt and pepper. Place the duck in a heavy casserole and roast it at 230°C for 20–30 minutes, turning every 10 minutes. Pour off the fat and take the duck out of the casserole. Add olive oil to casserole with the onion, garlic, pepper, thyme and sugar, and stir fry for 1–2 minutes. Add duck and pour in port or Madeira, then chicken stock, lemon juice and mushrooms. Cover tightly and simmer for 1 hour. Skim off any fat and add olives. Bring to the boil and whisk in cornflour mixed with a little water. Taste and season with salt and pepper. Serve with baked potatoes and a green salad.

Coconut curry (serves 4)

50 ml vegetable oil
1 onion, chopped
4 cloves garlic, finely chopped
3 T freshly chopped ginger
4 green chillies, finely chopped
½ t sugar
1 t turmeric
4 t ground cumin
½ t ground fenugreek
½ t ground cinnamon
400 ml coconut cream
600 g raw boneless chicken cut into 5-cm dice
salt
2 T fresh coriander leaves
1 t garam masala

Heat oil in a frying pan. Add onion, garlic, ginger and chillies, and stir fry until golden brown and soft. Do not burn. Add sugar and spices, except garam masala and coriander leaves. Stir fry on a low heat for 1 minute but do not burn. Add coconut cream and bring to the boil.

Pan fry chicken until browned, and then add it to the coconut sauce and simmer until cooked through. Taste and season with salt. Serve sprinkled with coriander leaves and garam masala.

Roasts, Sautées and Barbecues

Chicken roasted with butter *(serves 4)*

salt and pepper
1 t chopped fresh tarragon
50 g butter
1.5-kg roasting chicken

Preheat oven to 200°C. Mix salt, pepper, tarragon and butter, and put inside bird. Place chicken in roasting dish on its side and put into the oven. Turn the chicken over after 20 minutes and again after another 20 minutes. Baste frequently. After 1 hour, take chicken out of oven and serve with the juices from the pan as the sauce.

Chicken roasted with lemon, rosemary and white wine *(serves 4)*

1.5-kg chicken
1 large sprig rosemary
1 small lemon, quartered
50 g butter
salt and pepper
small knob butter
1 T flour
150 ml white wine
50 ml chicken stock or water
lemon juice
1 T chopped parsley

Stuff the chicken with rosemary, lemon quarters, butter, salt and pepper. Roast as for chicken roasted with butter (above). When the chicken is cooked, take it out of the roasting dish and discard lemon and rosemary. Keep hot. Pour fat out of roasting dish. Place the pan on the heat and add a small knob of butter. When it has melted, sprinkle in the flour and stir well with a wooden spoon. Pour in wine and stock, and stir vigorously. Bring to the boil and cook for 3–4 minutes until the gravy thickens. Taste and season with salt, pepper and lemon juice. Sprinkle in the parsley and serve separately.

Chicken roasted with cream cheese, garlic and tarragon *(serves 4)*

2 cloves garlic, chopped
1 T chopped fresh tarragon
½ c cream cheese
1 small onion, finely chopped
25 g butter
1.5-kg chicken
50 ml dry white wine or vermouth
100 ml chicken stock or water

Preheat oven to 200°C. Mix together garlic, tarragon, cream cheese, onion and butter and stuff the chicken with the mixture. Roast for 1 hour, basting frequently. When the chicken is cooked, take it out of the roasting dish and keep it hot. Pour off the fat from the roasting dish and scrape the cream cheese stuffing out of the chicken and put it in the roasting dish over moderate heat. Add the wine or vermouth, the chicken stock or water, and whisk vigorously. Bring to the boil and reduce by fast boiling until the sauce has thickened. Taste and season with salt and pepper. Carve the chicken and arrange it on a serving dish. Pour the sauce over.

Baby chicken roasted with sage

Stuffing per bird

½ c fresh breadcrumbs
1 T chopped fresh sage (dried will not do)
1 T chopped onion
1 t butter, softened
1 T chopped parsley
4 T dry white wine
salt and pepper

450-g baby chicken per person
2 rashers fat bacon per bird

Preheat oven to 200°C. Mix stuffing ingredients together and stuff the chickens. Wrap bacon securely around each bird and roast for 45 minutes, basting frequently. Serve with a little melted butter or vinaigrette, to which a finely chopped gherkin and spring onions have been added.

Chicken stuffed with dried fruit *(serves 4)*

This stuffing is also good for boned chicken and legs, and for turkey.

300 g dried apricots
300 g pitted prunes
1 onion, finely chopped
50 g butter
2 apples, cored, peeled and chopped
1 sprig fresh thyme
juice and rind 1 orange
2 T butter, melted

Cover apricots and prunes with boiling water and soak for 1 hour. Drain and chop. Preheat oven to 170°C. Gently fry onion in the 50 g butter until golden, then add apples, apricots, prunes, thyme and grated orange rind. Stir fry gently for 3 minutes. Season with salt and pepper, and spoon the mixture inside the chicken. Sew or skewer the bird closed. Put chicken in a roasting dish, pour on orange juice and melted butter, and roast for 1½ hours or until the chicken is tender. Serve with rice.

Chicken roasted with tomato and anchovies *(serves 4)*

50 g butter
6 anchovy fillets, mashed
1 large clove garlic, chopped
1 small onion, finely chopped
2 T chopped parsley
1.5-kg chicken
425-g can whole peeled tomatoes in juice
50 ml white wine
50 ml chicken stock or water
1 t sugar
salt and pepper

Preheat oven to 200°C. Mash together butter, anchovies, garlic, onion and parsley, and spread half of it over the chicken breast. Put the other half inside the chicken. Mash the tomatoes and mix with wine, stock, sugar, salt and pepper, and pour around the chicken. Roast for 1 hour, basting frequently with the tomato mixture. The tomatoes will cook down to a thick purée and this is the sauce. When the chicken is cooked, carve it and put it on a serving dish. Give the tomato mixture a good stir and pour it over the chicken. Serve with rice or pasta and grated Parmesan cheese.

Poulet à la Basquaise *(serves 4)*

1.5-kg chicken
salt and pepper
50 ml olive oil
1 onion, sliced
2 cloves garlic, chopped
1 red capsicum, sliced
5 cm-long piece peppercorn salami or one chorizo sausage, diced
2 T chopped parsley
1 t sugar
425-g can whole peeled tomatoes in juice

Preheat oven to 200°C. Season chicken with salt and pepper. In a roasting pan, heat the olive oil until hot but not smoking. Add onion, garlic, capsicum, salami, parsley and sugar. Stir fry without browning until the onion is transparent. Remove from heat and put the chicken in the middle of the onion mixture. Surround with mashed tomatoes. Roast for 1 hour, basting frequently. Serve with plain boiled rice with a generous knob of butter stirred through it.

Ms Lane's baked chicken breasts with watercress mousse *(serves 4)*

4 boneless chicken breasts (halves)
1 bunch watercress, well washed, thick stalks discarded, and very finely chopped
1 T grated Parmesan cheese
1 egg white, beaten
200 ml dry white wine
extra watercress

Sauce

150 ml plain yoghurt
2 egg yolks, beaten
grated rind 1 lemon
½ t turmeric

Preheat oven to 180°C. Skin chicken breasts (retaining skin) and beat until very thin. Mince or finely chop the skin and add to the watercress, Parmesan and egg white. Season well with salt and pepper and spread a quarter on each chicken breast. Roll up each breast and pack side by side into a smallish buttered casserole. Sprinkle the wine on, cover and bake for 30 minutes.

Meanwhile, in a double boiler, combine sauce ingredients and stir until hot and thickening. Taste and season with salt and pepper. Take the chicken breasts out of the casserole and arrange on a bed of watercress on a serving dish. Serve the sauce separately.

Chicken roasted with pork and prunes *(serves 4)*

300 g pitted prunes soaked for 1 hour in boiling water
150 g belly pork, minced
2 T chopped parsley
1 chicken liver, finely chopped
2 spring onions, finely chopped
25 g butter
1 carrot, peeled and cut into 1-cm dice
1 stalk celery, peeled and cut into 1-cm dice
½ c sliced mushrooms
1 onion, finely chopped
2 c white wine

Sauce
25 g butter
2 t flour
500 ml chicken stock
150 ml cream

Preheat oven to 200°C. Drain the prunes and chop half of them. Set the other half to one side. Mix together chopped prunes, pork, chopped parsley, liver and spring onions. Season well with salt and pepper and stuff the chicken with this mixture. In a deep metal casserole, melt 25 g butter and add the carrot, celery, mushrooms and onion. Stir fry for 3–4 minutes over a moderate heat until the vegetables have softened. Add wine and push the chicken into the middle of the vegetables. Cover and bake for 1 hour. Take the lid off for the last 20 minutes and baste frequently so the chicken browns.

Sauce: Melt the butter in a small saucepan, add the flour, and stir well. Pour in the stock, whisking vigorously to avoid lumps. Season well with salt and pepper. Simmer for 5 minutes. Set to one side. When the chicken is cooked, carve it and arrange it on a serving dish with the stuffing. Purée the vegetables from the roasting dish and discard any excess fat. Return the vegetables to the roasting dish, add the cream and the remaining prunes. Stir well. Bring to the boil and simmer for 3 minutes. Taste and season if necessary.

Chicken baked in salt *(serves 2)*

2 x 450-g baby chickens
12 cloves garlic, outer skin removed but not peeled
1.5 kg gros sel (coarse salt)

Preheat oven to 200°C. Line a roasting tin with foil and cover with 2–3 cm of salt. Press down well and push garlic cloves into the salt. Lay chickens on top and cover with remaining salt. Press down well. Bake for 45 minutes. Lift foil out onto a serving dish and crack open the salt ''crust''. Lift chicken out.

Serve with green beans and small baked potatoes in their jackets. Dress the potatoes with some of the cooked garlic cloves mashed with unsalted butter.

Grilled or barbecued marinated chicken

Here are two marinades for a 1-kg roasting chicken.

juice 2 lemons
1 T crushed black peppercorns
50 ml olive oil

Cut chicken down the backbone and open out flat. Crack the leg and wing joints so they will stay flat and give the whole chicken a pounding with a meat flattener to make sure it does.

Mix lemon juice, peppercorns and oil together, pour over chicken and marinate for 2–3 hours. Baste occasionally. Cook under a hot grill or barbecue for 35–40 minutes. Turn every 10 minutes.

2 t coriander seeds
seeds from 6 cardamom pods
1 T very finely chopped ginger
25 g butter
1 T oil

Fry coriander seeds over a high heat until they are well roasted. Mix or pound all ingredients to a paste and push under the skin of the flattened chicken. Set aside for 2–3 hours and then cook on the grill of the barbecue for 35–40 minutes. Turn every 10 minutes.

Pot roasted spiced chicken *(serves 4)*

1.5-kg chicken
50 g butter

Paste

1 T fresh coriander leaves
1 T freshly ground black pepper
seeds from 6 cardamom pods
½ t ground cloves
1 T fresh ginger
1 t salt
1 T garam marsala
50 g butter
juice 1 lemon

Mix all the paste ingredients in a blender, or pound until smooth. Spread half inside the chicken and half under the skin of the breast and legs. Melt the butter in a deep metal casserole and add the chicken on its side. Cover and cook at 200°C for 1 hour, turning the chicken halfway through. Uncover and turn the chicken onto its back for the last 10 minutes. Serve with lemon wedges and juices from the pan.

Gulam Rasool's Kashmiri chicken (p.45)

Basic roast duck *(serves 4)*

This method of roasting duck is one we use in restaurant cookery. It ensures a good flavour and releases the maximum amount of fat, which is important when cooking commercially raised ducks.

1 duck
1 carrot, chopped
1 stick celery, chopped
1 onion, skin on, roughly chopped
1 sprig parsley
1 clove garlic, crushed
50 ml dry white wine
water
1½ T flour mixed with
1 T butter

Preheat oven to 180°C. Cut any excess skin and fat off the duck. Discard the giblets but keep the neck. In a roasting dish, make a bed of the carrot, celery, onion, parsley, garlic and duck neck. Place the duck in the middle of the vegetables, breast down. Add the wine and fill the pan with water 6–8 cm deep. Put in oven and cook for 1 hour. Turn over and cook for another 45 minutes, basting frequently. Make sure the skin on the breast is crisp and golden. When the duck is cooked, take it out of the pan and keep it hot.

There should be quite a lot of fat on the surface of the liquid. Skim this off and discard the vegetables. Put the stock in the pan and bring it to the boil. Crumble in the flour and butter mixture, whisking all the time to avoid lumps. Boil until thickened to a gravy consistency. Taste and season with salt and pepper. Carve the duck and serve the sauce separately.

Duck with lychees and ginger

Follow the basic roast duck recipe but put 1 T finely chopped fresh ginger in with the vegetables and discard it with them when you skim off the fat. Pour in 150 ml of juice from the canned lychees and add 1 t redcurrant jelly. Bring to the boil and add 1 c lychees. Thicken as usual with flour and butter. Carve the duck and pour the sauce over it.

Duck with cherries and port (p.66)

Duck with cherries and port *(photograph opposite p.65)*

Follow the basic roast duck recipe (p.65) but add 100 ml port and 100 ml cherry juice if preserved cherries are used. If not, just the port. Then add the water to 6–8 cm depth. Take duck out, skim off fat, discard vegetables and bring to the boil. Reduce the volume of liquid by one quarter by fast boiling. Add 1 T redcurrant jelly and 1 c cherries (preserved or fresh). Thicken with flour and butter. If the sauce is too thick, thin with a little more port. Carve the duck. Pour the sauce over it and serve.

Duck with peaches or apricots

Roast duck as basic recipe (p.65), but add 100 ml medium sherry and water to 6–8 cm depth. Skim off fat, discard vegetables and bring to the boil. Reduce by a quarter by fast boiling. Add 1 T apricot jam and 1 c fresh peach or apricot slices. Cook for 3–4 minutes and thicken with flour and butter. Season with salt and pepper. Pour over carved duck.

Duck with apple and green peppercorns

Roast duck as basic recipe (p.65), but add 150 ml dry cider and water to make 6–8 cm depth. Skim fat and discard vegetables. Reduce liquid by a quarter by fast boiling. Add 1 c raw apple slices and 1 T green peppercorns. Cook for 3–4 minutes until apple is soft, then thicken with flour and butter. Season with salt and pepper. Serve over carved duck.

Duck with anise and honey

Roast duck as basic recipe (p.65), but add 2 star anise to the vegetable mixture. Take out duck, skim off fat, discard vegetables and anise. Add 1 large T strongly flavoured honey (Manuka is a good choice). Thicken with flour and butter if necessary. Taste and season with salt and pepper. Serve sauce over the carved duck.

Duck with red pepper and mushrooms

Roast duck as basic recipe (p.65), but substitute 150 ml red wine for the 50 ml white wine. Add 1 t sugar to the liquid in the roasting pan, and an extra clove of garlic. Take the duck out when it is cooked, skim off the fat and discard the vegetables. To the duck liquid add 2 c sliced mushrooms and 2 large red capsicums that have been skinned by burning them black all over under a grill or over a gas jet. Wash under cold water so that burnt skin comes off. Discard the core and seeds and slice them thinly. Thicken the sauce with flour and butter, and season with salt and pepper. Pour over the carved duck. Serve with plain rice.

Pheasant roasted with red wine, mushrooms and bacon *(serves 4)*

50 g butter
1 pheasant
150 ml red wine
½ onion, finely sliced
3 rashers bacon, chopped
2 c sliced mushrooms
1 T flour
250 ml chicken stock

Preheat oven to 190°C. Place butter inside the pheasant and roast in a smallish dish for 30 minutes. Pour on the red wine and roast for another 30 minutes, basting frequently. Remove the pheasant from the dish and keep it hot. Skim any fat off the juices in the pan and place the pan over a moderate heat. Add onion and bacon, and cook for 2–3 minutes, then add mushrooms and stir well. Cook for 1 minute, then sprinkle in the flour. Add the stock and stir well to avoid lumps of flour. Bring to the boil and cook for 2–3 minutes until the sauce thickens. Taste and season with salt and pepper. Carve the pheasant and pour the sauce over it.

Pheasant with red cabbage, prunes and bacon *(serves 4)*

1 pheasant
50 g butter
glass white wine
1 small red cabbage, cored and thinly sliced

50 g butter
½ onion, finely chopped
1 clove garlic, crushed
2 rashers bacon, chopped
1 sprig fresh thyme
1 bay leaf
juice and rind 1 orange
12 pitted prunes
50 ml white wine

Preheat oven to 190°C. Roast the pheasant in the butter for 1 hour, basting frequently so bird does not dry out. When cooked, remove it from the pan and make gravy in the usual way, adding a glass of white wine.

Put the red cabbage into a china or glass bowl and sprinkle a handful of salt over it. Stir well so the salt is evenly distributed through the cabbage. Leave for 1–2 hours, then wash well in cold running water. Shake dry and set aside. Melt the butter in a deep saucepan, add the onion, garlic, bacon, thyme and bay leaf, and stir fry over moderate heat until the onion is soft. Add the orange rind and juice and boil. Add cabbage, prunes and wine. Bring to the boil again and season well with freshly ground pepper (the cabbage will probably be salty enough). Cover tightly and simmer over a low heat for 25–30 minutes.

Arrange the cabbage in a serving dish. Put the carved pheasant on top and pour the gravy over everything.

Roast pheasant with cream, grapes and blue cheese *(serves 4)*

1 carrot, finely diced
1 stick celery, finely diced
1 onion, finely chopped
100 g butter, melted
1 pheasant
1 c black and white grapes, halved and seeded
1 T butter
100 ml chicken stock
200 ml dry white wine
100 ml cream
juice ½ lemon
salt and pepper
½ c good blue cheese (N.Z. blue vein, Stilton, Gorgonzola)

Preheat oven to 200°C. Put the carrot, celery and onion in a casserole dish, add melted butter. Put pheasant on top and roast for 1 hour until the pheasant is tender but not dry. Baste frequently. Meanwhile, gently stew the grapes in 1 T butter over a low heat for 3 minutes. Set to one side.

When the pheasant is cooked, remove from the casserole and keep hot. Place the casserole over a moderate heat and when it is hot, pour in the stock and wine. Stir well, scraping the caramelised bits off the casserole. Bring to the boil and add the cream. Boil again and taste; season with lemon juice, salt and pepper. Strain the sauce and add stewed grapes. Carve the pheasant and arrange on a serving dish. Pour the sauce over it and crumble the cheese over everything. Serve with fresh egg noodles that have been cooked in plenty of salted water, with a large knob of butter stirred through them at the last minute.

Roast pheasant stuffed with red onions and mozzarella *(serves 4)*

Stuffing

½ c fresh brown breadcrumbs
1 c mozzarella cheese, cut into 1-cm dice
1 red onion, finely chopped
50 g melted butter
1 T chopped parsley
1 clove garlic, finely chopped
grated rind ½ lemon

1 pheasant
100 g butter
1 t flour
wineglass of Marsala

Preheat oven to 190°C. Mix all the stuffing ingredients together and stuff the pheasant. Roast in the butter for 1 hour, basting frequently. When the pheasant is cooked, remove from the pan and sprinkle in the flour. Bring to the boil and add Marsala. Taste and season well with salt and pepper. Serve sauce separately from the carved pheasant and stuffing.

Stir fried chicken and vegetables *(serves 4)*

¼ c sesame oil
3-cm piece fresh ginger, very finely sliced
2 cloves garlic, chopped
2 green chillies, thinly sliced
2 whole boneless chicken breasts, sliced finely
100 g green beans, sliced
1 large red capsicum, cored, seeded and finely sliced
2 carrots, thinly sliced
1½ c broccoli tops
1 c button mushrooms
1 T honey
4 T sherry
4 T soy sauce

Heat the oil in a wok or frying pan. When it is hot, add ginger, garlic and chillies and cook for 1 minute. Add chicken and stir fry until it is golden. Add vegetables and stir fry for 1 minute. When they are hot, add honey, sherry and soy sauce, and continue stir frying until the vegetables are "al dente" (cooked but still crisp). Season well with salt and pepper, and serve with rice or noodles.

Chicken sautéed with mushrooms and baby onions *(serves 4)*

1.5-kg chicken, jointed
seasoned flour
100 g butter
1 clove garlic, finely chopped
1 T chopped tarragon
16 baby onions, peeled, or 3 medium onions, finely sliced
2 c sliced mushrooms
200 ml dry white wine
150 ml cream
salt and pepper
lemon juice
1 T chopped parsley

Roll the chicken in the seasoned flour. Heat the butter in a heavy pan and sauté over a moderate heat until golden brown. Remove chicken and set aside. Add garlic, tarragon and onions, and stir fry until the onion is golden brown. Add mushrooms and chicken. Stir carefully and add wine. Bring to the boil, cover and simmer for 25 minutes. Remove chicken to a serving dish and keep hot. Add cream to pan and reduce by fast boiling until the sauce is thick enough to coat a spoon. Taste and season with salt, pepper and lemon juice. Pour the sauce over the chicken pieces and sprinkle with parsley. Serve with rice.

Panfried crumbed chicken breasts

boneless half chicken breasts, skinned
flour
egg beaten with a little milk
breadcrumbs
oil or butter for frying

Roll the breasts in flour, then egg and milk, and then breadcrumbs. Pan fry in shallow oil or butter, or a mixture of both, until they are golden brown, then put the frying pan into a hot oven to finish cooking. It takes about 10 minutes. This way, the chicken cooks through without burning. Serve with one of the sauces in the sauce chapter.

However, the breasts can also be stuffed with one of the following stuffings. First gently beat out the flap of flesh on the inside of the breast. Cut a small pocket in the thick part of the flesh in the main part so the flattened flap will fold over and cover the opening. Stuff the incision and fold the flesh over it and crumb as described above.

Avocado and cream cheese filling

1 avocado
½ c cream cheese
juice ½ lemon
1 spring onion, finely sliced

Mash everything together, season with salt and pepper, and stuff 4 breasts. Crumb and cook as in the basic recipe. Good with sauce hollandaise (p.20) or tomato salsa (p.18).

Ricotta and herb stuffing

1 c ricotta cheese
1 clove garlic, finely chopped
1 T finely chopped mixed fresh herbs

Mix together, season with salt and pepper, and stuff 4 breasts. Crumb and cook as in the basic recipe.

Cream cheese and coriander

1 c cream cheese
2 T coarsely chopped fresh coriander
1 T green peppercorns
2 cloves garlic, chopped

Mix together, season with salt and pepper, and stuff 4 breasts. Crumb and cook as in the basic recipe. Good with tomato salsa (p.18).

Prawn and garlic butter

½ c cooked prawns, finely chopped
½ c well flavoured garlic butter
½ t paprika
good pinch cayenne pepper

Mix together, season with salt, pepper and lemon juice, and stuff 4 breasts. Crumb and cook as in the basic recipe. Serve with sauce remoulade (p.20).

Chicken sautéed with vegetables *(serves 4)*

1.5-kg chicken, jointed
seasoned flour
50 g butter
3 T olive oil
2 cloves garlic, finely chopped
1 T chopped fresh marjoram or oregano
2 T chopped parsley
1 large onion, finely chopped
1 t sugar
1 carrot, cut into 1-cm dice
1 stalk celery, cut into thin strips
2 courgettes, thinly sliced
2 green capsicum, finely sliced
½ c green olives
150 ml dry white wine
425-g can whole peeled tomatoes in juice, mashed

Roll the chicken pieces in the seasoned flour. In a large heavy frying pan melt the butter, add oil and when it is hot, brown the chicken over a moderate heat. Remove chicken. To the pan add garlic, marjoram or oregano, parsley, onion, sugar, carrot and celery. Stir fry until the onion is golden. Do not let the mixture burn. Add the courgettes, capsicum and olives. and stir fry for another 4 minutes. Add chicken and wine and stir well. Bring to the boil and add tomatoes. Boil again and simmer for 20 minutes until the chicken is tender. Taste and season well with salt and pepper. Serve with rice.

Sautéed chicken livers with tomato and Parmesan *(serves 4)*

4 T clarified butter
2 c chicken livers, trimmed and cleaned
1 clove garlic, chopped
1 onion, finely chopped
1 T flour
100 ml Marsala
100 ml dry white wine
4 tomatoes, peeled, seeded, cored and roughly chopped
½ c freshly grated Parmesan cheese

Heat the clarified butter in a heavy frying pan until it is smoking. Carefully add the chicken livers and turn them over a few times so they are sealed. Add garlic and onion and reduce the heat to moderate. Stir fry the livers, onion and garlic until the onion is golden. Sprinkle on the flour and stir well. Add Marsala and wine and stir well. Add tomatoes and simmer for 4 minutes. Taste and season with salt and pepper. Sprinkle on the Parmesan and put under a hot grill until the cheese browns. Serve on croutons of French bread, and accompany with a salad.

Sautéed chicken livers with grapes *(serves 4)*

50 ml clarified butter
2 c chicken livers, trimmed and cleaned
50 ml brandy
4 spring onions, finely chopped
1 T flour
1 T chopped parsley
juice ½ lemon
150 ml chicken stock
1 c grapes, seeded (cut in half if necessary)
50 ml cream

Heat the clarified butter until it is smoking. Carefully add the livers and turn them a few times so they are sealed. Reduce the heat and add brandy. Set it alight and when the flames have died down, add spring onions and stir fry for 1 minute. Add flour and stir well. Add parsley, lemon juice and chicken stock, and stir well to avoid lumps. Cook for 3 minutes. If the sauce gets too thick, thin with a little more chicken stock. It should be the consistency of cream. Add the grapes and cream. Cook for 1 minute, taste and season with salt and pepper. Serve with buttered rice.

Sautéed chicken livers with bacon and mushrooms *(serves 4)*

50 ml clarified butter
2 c chicken livers, trimmed and cleaned
1 onion, finely chopped
1 clove garlic, finely chopped
½ c chopped bacon
1 c sliced mushrooms
1 T flour
100 ml port
100 ml chicken stock

Heat the clarified butter until smoking and carefully add the livers. Turn them over several times to seal them. Reduce the heat, add onion, garlic and bacon, and stir until the onion is golden. Add mushrooms and cook for 2 minutes. Sprinkle on the flour and stir well. Pour in the port and boil. Add stock and boil again. Simmer for 4–5 minutes, adding more stock if the sauce gets too thick. Taste and season with salt and pepper. Serve on thick slices of toasted French bread.

Sautéed chicken livers with shallots *(serves 4)*

50 ml clarified butter
2 c chicken livers, trimmed and cleaned
1 c finely chopped shallots
2 T chopped parsley
2 t green peppercorns
150 ml dry white wine
100 ml cream
juice ½ lemon

Heat the clarified butter until it is smoking and carefully add the livers. Turn several times to seal them. Reduce heat, add shallots, parsley and green peppercorns. Stir fry over a gentle heat until the shallots are golden. Turn up heat, add wine and boil for 2 minutes. Add cream and lemon juice, and boil for 3 minutes. Taste and season with salt and pepper. Serve with toasted slices of French bread.

Sautéed chicken livers with lime and ginger *(serves 4)*

Marinade

½ c fresh lime juice
1 T finely chopped fresh ginger
½ t freshly ground pepper
1 t paprika
2 cloves garlic, chopped
½ t salt
1 t sugar

2 c chicken livers, trimmed and cleaned
50 g butter

Mix together marinade ingredients and marinate chicken livers for 1–2 hours.

Melt butter in a heavy frying pan. When it is hot but not brown, add the drained livers. Stir fry over a moderate heat until the livers are cooked but still pink inside; about 5–6 minutes. Add reserved marinade and a generous knob of butter. Stir well and serve over rice.

Marinated quails

Two quails per person is enough. Cut them through lengthways so you have two identical halves. Cut out the back bone, slide the knife under the rib cage and cut it away. This deals with all the bones that make eating quail so tedious. All you have left are the wing and leg bones.

Marinade 1

50 ml olive oil
100 ml red wine
½ finely sliced onion
1 clove garlic, crushed
6 juniper berries, crushed
1 t sugar or honey
few turns of the pepper mill

Mix ingredients together and marinate the quail halves for at least 2 hours (overnight is better). Drain and fry until crisp in hot olive oil. Serve with slices of French bread fried in olive oil, and good French mustard. Excellent grilled on the barbecue.

Marinade 2

150 ml yoghurt
3 cloves garlic, crushed
juice 1 lemon
½ t salt
1 t fresh coriander
1 t ground cumin
pinch cayenne pepper

Mix ingredients together and marinate quail halves overnight. Next day, wipe off the marinade. Fry quail in hot olive oil and serve with almond rice pilau (opposite).

Almond rice pilau

250 g long grain rice (Basmati, if possible)
50 g butter
½ t salt
½ t turmeric
1 t fresh chopped ginger
1 t garam marsala
1 onion, finely chopped
½ c currants
⅔ c flaked almonds
freshly ground pepper
100 ml dry white wine
200 ml water
knob of butter
yoghurt mixed with chopped mint, lemon juice and salt

Wash rice well and soak for at least 1 hour in cold water. Drain.

Preheat oven to 200°C. Melt butter in a metal casserole. Add salt, turmeric, ginger, garam marsala and onion. Stir fry over a moderate heat until onion is golden. Add currants, almonds and a few turns of the pepper mill. Stir fry for 2 minutes. Add rice and stir well. Add wine and water, and bring to the boil. Cover tightly with a lid or tinfoil and cook in the oven for 25 minutes. Do not lift the lid or the steam will escape and the rice will not cook. Remove from the oven. Stir in generous knob of butter and serve with the quails on top. Serve the yoghurt mixture in a separate dish. Elegant and delicious.

Indian marinated chicken *(serves 4)*

A variation on Tandoori chicken (for which one needs a Tandoor oven) that can be made in a domestic oven.

1.5-kg chicken, jointed, skinned, and pricked all over

Marinade

300 ml plain unsweetened yoghurt
1 t salt
juice 1 lemon
½ onion chopped
1 clove garlic
1 T fresh chopped ginger
½ t cayenne pepper
1 T garam marsala
1 t ground cumin

Blend all marinade ingredients until smooth. Pour onto the chicken pieces and marinate overnight.

Preheat oven to its highest heat. Shake off any excess marinade from the chicken pieces, place in a shallow baking dish and bake for 20–25 minutes. Serve with plain rice and salad.

Dry chicken and coconut curry *(serves 4)*

50 ml ghee or clarified butter
1 clove garlic, chopped
1 green chilli, finely chopped
1 T ground cumin
1 T finely chopped fresh ginger
½ t turmeric
1 t salt
1 t ground black pepper
1 onion, chopped
3 c diced chicken meat, skinned
1 c desiccated coconut
1 c chopped fresh coriander leaves
½ c lemon juice

Heat the ghee or clarified butter in a heavy frying pan until it is hot. Add garlic, chilli, cumin, ginger, turmeric, salt and pepper. Stir fry without burning for 1 minute. Add onion and stir fry for 1 minute. Add chicken and stir fry for 5 minutes, then add coconut, coriander and lemon juice. Stir well and continue cooking over a gentle heat until the chicken is cooked. Serve with rice and a bowl of yoghurt.

Indian baked chicken and onions *(serves 4)*

100 ml oil
1 t salt
4 cloves garlic, finely chopped
1 T finely chopped fresh ginger
1 T ground coriander
1 T ground cumin
½ t ground turmeric
½ t cayenne pepper
½ t garam marsala
4 onions, very finely sliced
1.5-kg chicken, jointed
3 tomatoes, peeled, seeded, cored and thinly sliced

Preheat oven to 200°C. In a large frying pan, heat half the oil until it is hot. Add salt, garlic, ginger, coriander, cumin, turmeric, cayenne and garam marsala. Reduce the heat and stir fry gently for 1 minute. Add onions and gently stir fry for another 5 minutes. Remove from heat and put spice and onion mixture into a metal casserole. Set aside.

Heat the remaining oil in the frying pan and brown the chicken. Put the chicken on top of the onion mixture and sprinkle tomatoes over it. Cover tightly, bake for 40 minutes until the chicken is tender and the vegetables a thick purée.

Yakitori (Japanese chicken kebabs) *(serves 4)*

8 chicken livers, trimmed and cleaned
2 whole chicken breasts, skinned, boned and cut into bite-sized pieces
4 spring onions, cut into 3-cm lengths

Marinade

1 T very finely sliced fresh ginger
½ c soy sauce
½ c mirin or sherry
1 T sugar

Mix all marinade ingredients together and marinate chicken livers for at least 6 hours at room temperature. Drain. Cut livers in half and thread 4 halves onto each of 4 sate sticks. Now thread the chicken alternatively with the spring onions onto saté skewers until the chicken and spring onion is used up.

Barbecue or grill the chicken and chicken liver kebabs over a high heat, painting them liberally with the marinade as they cook. Sprinkle with freshly ground black pepper. Serve with plain, boiled, shortgrain rice and the following salad.

Salad

1 carrot, cut into very thin strips
2 spring onions cut into very thin strips
1 telegraph cucumber cut into very thin strips
4 radishes cut into very thin strips
1 buttercup lettuce
1 small can crab meat, drained

Soak the vegetables in iced water for 1 hour. Drain. Wash the lettuce and arrange on a shallow bowl. Make a heap of the crab meat on top and sprinkle with the vegetables. Serve with the following dressing.

Dressing

4 T sesame seeds
½ c mayonnaise (p.19)
pinch cayenne pepper
1 T soy sauce
5 T rice vinegar
4 T dashi (this is bonito soup made from dried bonito flakes available from Japanese grocers)

Cook sesame seeds over a high heat in a dry frying pan until they brown and pop. Cool. Mix all ingredients together and serve with the salad.

Indian lemon baked chicken *(serves 4)*

1.5-kg chicken
1 lemon, cut into 3-cm dice, skin on
juice 2 lemons
2 cloves garlic
2 T chopped fresh ginger
1 t ground cumin
1 T ground coriander
100 g butter, softened
2 T black mustard seeds

Preheat oven to 200°C. Wash chicken well and pat dry with kitchen paper. Prick all over with a sharp knife. Stuff the chopped lemon inside. Put the lemon juice, garlic, ginger, cumin and coriander into a blender and blend to a cream. Add the butter and blend till smooth. Rub the mixture all over the chicken and sprinkle on the mustard seeds. Wrap the chicken in a large piece of tinfoil so it is sealed. Bake for 1½ hours until chicken is tender.

Indonesian baked chicken *(serves 4)*

50 g butter
2 cloves garlic, chopped
2 onions, finely sliced
1 t sugar
1 t sambal oelek
½ c soy sauce
juice ½ lemon
1.5-kg chicken, jointed

Preheat oven to 175°C. Melt butter in a deep casserole and fry garlic and onion over a moderate heat until the onion is golden. Add sugar, sambal, soy sauce and lemon juice, and stir well. Put chicken pieces on top. Cover tightly and bake for 2 hours. When the chicken is cooked, crisp the skin under a hot grill and serve.

Chicken kofta *(makes 12 small patties)*

These are Indian chicken rissoles. Good for snacks and parties.

500 g chicken meat
1 onion
2 red chillies
2 cloves garlic
2 spring onions
1 t coriander
½ t salt
1 egg

Mince the chicken, onion, chillies, garlic and spring onions in a processor until they are a paste. Add the other ingredients and mix well. Shape into small balls and fry in deep hot oil until golden and cooked through. Serve with lemon wedges, chutney, or in pita bread with lettuce and tomatoes.

Index